Hello, my friend.

Thank you for picking up this book and opening yourself to the possibility of living Fearless and Free. You hold a bit of my heart in your hands, and I hold prayers and hopes for you in my heart. We're connected through these pages, and I think that is a rare and precious privilege.

This eleven-week Bible study comes after a lot of soul-searching. It's been a personal journey, and I know it isn't over. God loves you and me too much to leave us where we are, and so He always calls us to a place of deeper healing. It's a long-term process, but that shouldn't discourage us. Each breakthrough is life-changing, meaning as we move along, life gets better and better. I think this approach to life sounds much more appealing than dreading and trying to avoid the inevitable process of aging. With every passing year, we should be growing in wholeness, wisdom, and peace. That is true beauty. *Fearless and Free* is your companion on this pilgrimage.

Some of what we'll be exploring are things I've known a long time—some of them for my whole life. Others I've learned recently. Here's the thing—as far back as I can remember, I have loved Jesus, and my faith has been incredibly important to me. I don't recall a time when I wasn't (however poorly) trying to follow Him. But even then, even growing up in an incredibly faith-filled home, even with years of studying the Bible, even with having taken my prayer life seriously for decades, there were critical things I was missing.

What I'm proposing to you in *Fearless and Free* is this:

If even one of these things that we are talking about is missing from your life, then you can lose sight of where you're going and who you are.

I have boiled it down to the things that I think are most essential for us to have straight, for us to be clear on. This is not the end of the road—there is so much more. But we need to understand and wrestle with these topics, or we will be at risk of truly missing out on who God created us to be.

You may be going through this Bible study on your own, with a small group of friends, or in a parish setting. All are fruitful ways to process this material. It is likely that some sacred and private emotions and memories will surface. It is my prayer that you will have people surrounding you who are equipped and trustworthy to manage what you might be led to share. But the truth is, very few small group leaders will be able to pastor you through the healing of deep wounds. This is soul work and is best done with a counselor. So I am praying that we all would be discerning about what things to share with a group, and what should be worked through with a professional.

Let's start peeling back the layers so we get to the core of who we are in Christ.

May He make us Fearless and Free ~

Lisa Brenninkmeyer
Founder and Chief Purpose Officer, Walking with Purpose

Fearless and Free

Experiencing Healing and Wholeness in Christ

www.walkingwithpurpose.com

Authored by Lisa Brenninkmeyer
Cover and page design by True Cotton
Production management by Christine Welsko

IMPRIMATUR   + William E. Lori, S.T.D., Archbishop of Baltimore

The recommended Bible translations for use in Blaze and Walking with Purpose studies are: The New American Bible, which is the translation used in the United States for the readings at Mass; The Revised Standard Version, Catholic Edition; and The Jerusalem Bible.

Any internet addresses (websites, blogs, etc.) in this book are offered as a resource and may change in the future. Please refer to www.walkingwithpurpose.com as the central location for corresponding materials and references.

Printed: June 2019

ISBN: 978-1-943173-26-6

Fearless and Free Eleven Week Bible Study

heart full of grace

TABLE OF CONTENTS

INTRODUCTION

LESSONS

APPENDICES

Welcome to Walking with Purpose

You have many choices when it comes to how you spend your time—thank you for choosing Walking with Purpose. Studying God's Word with an open and receptive heart will bring spiritual growth and enrichment to all aspects of your life, making every moment that you've invested well worth it.

Each one of us comes to this material from our own unique vantage point. You are welcome as you are. No previous experience is necessary. Some of you will find that the questions in this study cause you to think about concepts that are new to you. Others might find much is a review. God meets each one of us where we are, and He is always faithful, taking us to a deeper, better place spiritually, regardless of where we begin.

The Structure of *Fearless and Free*

Fearless and Free is an eleven-week Bible study that integrates Scripture with the teachings of the Roman Catholic Church to point us to principles that help us manage life's pace and pressure while living with calm and steadiness. It is designed for both interactive personal study and group discussion.

If you are going through *Fearless and Free* with a small group in your parish, you'll begin your session by discussing one of the lessons from the *Fearless and Free* Study Guide. Following the small group discussion, you'll gather to watch the accompanying video.

If you're going through this study either on your own or in a small group, you are welcome to order the DVDs, but you might find it simpler to watch the talks online. The URL for each talk is listed on the Talk outline within the study guide.

Study Guide Format and Reference Materials

The *Fearless and Free Study Guide* is divided into three sections:

The first section comprises eleven lessons. Most lessons are divided into five "days" to help you form a habit of reading and reflecting on God's Word regularly. If you are a woman who has only bits and pieces of time throughout your day to accomplish tasks, you will find this breakdown of the lessons especially helpful. Each day focuses on Scripture readings and related teaching passages, and ends with a Quiet Your Heart reflection. In addition, Day Five includes a lesson conclusion; a resolution section, in which you set a goal for yourself based on a theme of the lesson; and short clips from the *Catechism of the Catholic Church*, which are referenced throughout the lesson to complement the Scripture study.

For the talks in this series, accompanying outlines are offered as guides for taking notes. Included are questions to either use for personal reflection, or for additional small group discussion. URLs are also provided for those who would like to view the talks online.

The second section, the appendices, contains supplemental materials referred to during the study, and includes an article about Saint Thérèse of Lisieux, the patron saint of Walking with Purpose (Appendix 1). Appendix 7, *Scripture Memory*, gives instructions on how to memorize Scripture. A memory verse has been chosen for *Fearless and Free*, and we encourage you to memorize it as you move through the Bible study. An illustration of the verse can be found in Appendix 7, and a color version and phone lock screen can be downloaded from our website. Appendix 8 is a Small Group Leader's guide which provides additional insights into guiding women on the Fearless and Free journey.

The third section contains the answer key. You will benefit so much more from the Bible study if you work through the questions on your own, searching your heart, as this is your very personal journey of faith. The answer key is meant to enhance small group discussion and provide personal guidance or author's insight where needed.

At the end of the book are pages on which to write weekly prayer intentions.

Walking with Purpose™ Website

Please visit our website at www.walkingwithpurpose.com to find supplemental materials that complement our Bible studies; a link to our online store for additional Bible studies, DVDs, books, and more; and the following free content:

WWP Scripture Printables of our exclusively designed verse cards that complement all Bible studies. Available in various sizes, lock screens for phones, and a format that allows you to e-mail them to friends.

WWP Bible Study Playlists of Lisa's favorite music to accompany each Bible study.

WWP Videos of all Talks by Lisa Brenninkmeyer.

WWP Blog by Lisa Brenninkmeyer, a safe place where you are welcome, where the mask can drop and you can be real. Subscribe for updates.

WWP Leadership Development Program
We are here to help you take your leadership to the next level! Through our training, you'll discover insights that help you achieve your leadership potential. You'll be empowered to step out of your comfort zone and experience the rush of serving God with passion and purpose. We want you to know that you are not alone; we offer you encouragement and the tools you need to reach out to a world that desperately needs to experience the love of God. ·

Links to WWP Social Media

Twitter, Pinterest, Facebook, Instagram

 NOTES

With Gratitude

The insight and editing provided by these four remarkable people was invaluable in the writing of *Fearless and Free*:

To Sarah Kamienski ~ You met me when my heart was guarded, and you taught me that I can't self-protect and love at the same time. The only reason I could learn that critical truth from you was because you made it safe for me to share the raw and honest parts of my soul that I had kept hidden for a long time. Thank you for seeing me. Thank you for transforming my family with your guidance and insight. And thank you for caring about every single word of this Bible study and helping it to be so much better.

To Heather Khym ~ You are the one who got this whole ball rolling for me. When I traveled to your neck of the woods in Vancouver, B.C., I had no idea that I'd be embarking on a journey of healing. I didn't even know I needed it. Thank you for challenging me to slow down and step off the wheel of production in order to reflect, go deep, and stop living as a performing orphan. Your example and influence have changed me for good.

To Julie Ricciardi ~ You've always been the first one to work through what I write, and I treasure your feedback like it's gold. Thank you for asking me the hard questions, and for helping me to explain things as simply as possible. Most of all, thank you for taking the teachings of the WWP Bible studies and living them out in your own life. The transformation I have seen in you over the ten years of our friendship is a daily reminder of the beauty and strength that come from a life rooted in God's Word.

To Dr. Bob Schuchts ~ What Leo and I have learned from you has unlocked something within us both, and has led us to a place of more authentic and mature love. The Healing the Whole Person conference released a joy in me that I haven't experienced since childhood. Thank you, a million times over. Your belief that the teachings in *Fearless and Free* matter and are needed has meant the world to me. Your edits, with your sensitivity to the heart of the wounded, have made this study so much better.

NOTES

Lessons

NOTES

Walking with Purpose is a community of women growing in faith – together! This is where women are gathering. Join us!

www.walkingwithpurpose.com

Lesson 1

FREEDOM TALK

Accompanying talk can be viewed by DVD or digital download purchase or access online at walkingwithpurpose.com/videos.

I. THE WAKENING (Ephesians 1-3)

A. Awakening to our True Identity

"He chose us in Christ before the foundation of the world to be holy and blameless before Him in love. He destined us for adoption as His children through Jesus . . . Through Him we have redemption through His blood, the forgiveness of our trespasses, according to the riches of His grace." Ephesians 1:4-5, 7

"You did not choose me, I chose you." John 15:16

B. Awakening to Real Life

What kind of a life did He choose us for? Ephesians 1:4 tells us that He chose us for a _____ and _____ life.

The word *holy* comes from the Greek word *hagios*, which always brings to mind the idea of _____ and _____.

Blameless comes from the Greek word *amomos*. It's a sacrificial word, used to describe the unblemished animal sacrifice that could be offered to God. It means _____, _____, _____.

How can we be blameless?

This is the divine exchange—our _____ for *His* _____. Our _____for *His* _____.

11

II. THE WRESTLING (Ephesians 4-5)

    A. Wrestling with our Mind and Emotions

       Ephesians 4:17 challenges us to no longer live in "the futility of our minds." Instead, as it says in Ephesians 4:23–24, we are to "Be renewed in the Spirit of our minds and clothe ourselves with the new self."

       Our heavenly Father speaks hope, _____, _____, and_____ into our lives. The enemy speaks despair, _____, _____, and _____.

       Whose voice are you listening to?

    B. Tools and Weapons for Wrestling

III. THE WARRIOR (Ephesians 6)

    A. Our Warrior Mother

    B. Recognize the Battle

Discussion Questions

1. Where are you at in terms of joy, freedom, and contentment? Do any of these words or phrases describe you?

numb	discontented
tired	not enough
insignificant	perfectionist
burned out	powerless
trying to stay in control	yearning for more
inadequate	

2. Do you feel you walk in your true identity as a beloved daughter of God, or do you find yourself hustling to prove your worth and striving to earn God's love? Or have you given up because the road to holiness just feels too hard?

3. Which section are you most excited to dive into—the Wakening, the Wrestling, or the Warrior? Why?

Looking for more material? We've got you covered! Walking with Purpose meets women where they are in their spiritual journey. From our Opening Your Heart 22-lesson foundational Bible study to more advanced studies, we have something to help each and every woman grow closer to Christ. Find out more:

www.walkingwithpurpose.com

THE
Wakening

YOUR TRUE IDENTITY IN CHRIST

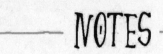

NOTES

Lesson 2

CHOSEN BIBLE STUDY

Introduction

"It takes courage to grow up and become who you really are." E. E. Cummings

The first step of our journey begins with the Wakening. My hope for this lesson is that we will wake up to who we really are and what we are worth.

We're coming to this material from all sorts of places. Some of us are hiding out. We've mastered the art of self-protection and are very careful about what parts of us we allow others to see. Others of us are running so fast to prove we are good enough that our hearts are racing. I wonder if you've started to disengage because it's the only way you know how to protect your heart. You might be caught in the web of perfectionism. Maybe you are addicted to change because it gives you an excuse for feeling untethered. Shame may be breathing hard down your neck. Perhaps you have settled for mediocrity. All of those things have been true of me, far more often than I'd care to admit.

One thing I know for sure: We all are full of emotions, and too many of us have been taught that they aren't worth anyone's attention, or at the very least, that those emotions need to be dealt with quietly, because nice girls know how to behave appropriately and graciously and not make a fuss. For too long, our spiritual lives have been divorced from our emotional lives. The result? We are living sterile, abbreviated versions of the lives God created us for. We end up cutting ourselves off from the tough or uncomfortable emotions that just might be gifts from God to entice us back to Him.

Can you remember who you were before you were told who you should be?

I am giving you permission to take the time to explore that. You are allowed to unravel, to come a little bit undone. Because that's what happens when we start to wake up. But make no mistake, the alternative is to stay sleepy and remain numb.

There may be a certain degree of comfort in that level of existence, but something is decidedly missing, and for me, that something was joy.

Sometimes the thing you are most afraid of doing is the very thing that will set you free. So Jesus is inviting you on this journey toward freedom—the Wakening. Your emotions, memories, hurts, and dreams are welcome here.

We are going to *pay attention* to our emotions, but we are not going to let them decide where we are going. They will reveal much to us and they matter immensely, but if we let them take the steering wheel, we'll end up on the road to victimhood.

Our compass is going to be Scripture. Our guide is going to be the only source of truth: Jesus. We are going to wrap our minds around our true identity, why we are here, and what part God plays in all of this. We are going to reclaim territory that the enemy of our souls has taken from us.

Are you ready, my friend? It's time to awaken and arise.

Day One
BELONGING

Read Ephesians 1:1–4.

1. A. Saint Paul begins in Ephesians 1:1 by telling us the two most important things to know about him: He was an **apostle of Jesus Christ** and he held that position **by the will of God**. Being an apostle of Jesus Christ meant that Saint Paul belonged to Christ. How did Saint Paul describe this reality in 1 Corinthians 6:19–20?

Later, we'll go deeper into what that means. For now, suffice it to say that Saint Paul knew he was not the one calling the shots. He was not his own. When God told Saint Paul to go, he went. The word *apostle* in the original Greek means "to send out." Saint Paul was a man with a mission, sent out by God.

When Paul went on to explain why he held that position, he didn't list his credentials. He simply said that it was by the will of God. Amazingly, God wanted *him*.

Why would Paul have found that hard to believe? Because of his past. A well-respected Jew with the pedigree and education to demand respect, Paul had been determined to protect the purity of the Jewish faith and way of life. The Christians threatened that, and he threw all his energy into persecuting them mercilessly. He stood and consented to the stoning of Saint Stephen, a devoted Christian and the first martyr. He tried to destroy the church, and entering house after house, dragged out men and women to send them to prison and to face possible execution. But an encounter with Jesus on the road to Damascus altered everything. Paul fell to the ground and came face-to-face with Jesus Himself, who asked him why he was persecuting Him. Temporarily literally blinded by the encounter, he was converted and became the greatest evangelizer and preacher of Christianity of all time. His beginning was not his end—not even close. In some ways, what could have been his end was actually his beginning.

Saint Paul certainly could have considered his past actions total deal breakers in terms of being a leader in the early Church. Yet somehow he was able to see himself as God saw him instead of allowing his past sins to define him.

B. I wonder where you are at today. Are you sitting with this Bible study in hand, feeling disqualified on some level? Do you look at your past and feel defined by your mistakes? Have you ever compared yourself to another woman and thought, "*She* is chosen; *she* belongs. God can use her. But me? That's another story"? Do you feel you don't belong?

What we have to remember is that it's not our credentials or perfection that qualify us to belong to Christ. Jesus Christ is drawing you to Him, right now, simply because He utterly adores you. You are His. He wants you. Don't just rush by these words. Pause. Give them a second to sink in, and marinate in this truth.

2. A. Ephesians 1:2 greets the readers with a prayer/wish for what two things?

Grace means "gift." It's a participation in the actual life of God. It describes the offering of undeserved mercy. It is unearned favor, originating in the heart of God. It is offered to us lavishly, but we have to choose to receive it. We have to empty our hands of our achievements and self-justifications in order to be able to accept grace from Him.

Peace, when used in Scripture, is not just describing the absence of trouble. It describes the presence of what is good. *Shalom*, translated *peace*, exists regardless of outward circumstances. It's a state of contentment and security, unaltered by chaos and suffering.

"Grace to you and peace." This is the order it goes in; we need the grace of God before we can experience His peace. Are you longing for peace? You can't skip that first step of receiving Christ's grace. We have a choice: to live a life of proving and hustling, or to live a life receiving the free gift of grace. We can't have it both ways.

B. In which area of your life are you longing for peace? Do you see yourself hustling to prove your worth or numbing out in order to try to find peace?

Ephesians 1:2 tells us that the grace and peace we are after come from only one source: God our Father and the Lord Jesus Christ. If we look for them anywhere else, we'll just end up disappointed and disillusioned.

3. According to Ephesians 1:4, what happened before the foundation of the world?

Deep within, we all have a desire to feel chosen. Yet many of us feel alone, unseen. This can be our experience even if we are surrounded by people. But there is a love that never fails, a love that chose you. You were chosen in Christ. He picked you. He sees you—not just as a member of humanity, but as an individual, unique, beautiful woman. You are wanted. Any thoughts swimming around in your head that suggest otherwise are not from God. You are His beloved.

He chose you for a purpose—to be set apart "in Christ." What does that mean? It means that as a daughter of God, you are united to Jesus ("you are in Christ") in such a way that everything He has is yours. You have a spiritual inheritance because of your union with Him. The fruits of the Holy Spirit (love, joy, peace, patience, kindness, goodness, faithfulness, gentleness, and self-control) are in you because of Him. He shares His Father and mother with you; you have inherited a family. The intimacy He always has experienced with God the Father? That is offered to you as well.

Quiet your heart and enjoy His presence. . . . You belong in Him.

On the day you were baptized, you were marked as a daughter of God. You are His. And then the journey began. On this journey, a lot of things have hurt you. Sometimes it's been because of another person's mistake; sometimes it's been your own. Your heart has been wounded. God has never wanted you to be hurt, and in fact desires your good more than you do.

God has chosen you, but He wants you to choose Him, too. This isn't something that just happens because you grew up in a certain Church or attended Mass regularly. I'm talking about a moment when you open up the door to Him. You don't need to clean yourself up or spend months debating the ins and outs of this. It can be the simplest thing in the world—a few words: "Jesus, please come." Even as I write this, He is there, waiting for you.

He is knocking on the door of your heart, but He is a gentleman. He won't force His way into your life. He waits to be invited in, to be asked to draw near. He knows you are wary of letting anyone that close, of being so vulnerable. At first, it might not seem easy to let Him see the real you—the fears, insecurity, sins, hurts, and questions. Would it help to know He already knows it all? He simply longs to have you share your heart with Him.

And here's the thing: Something can be true, even when it doesn't feel true. And this next truth is one of those things.

He is safe. He is the only one who will always be perfectly tender with your heart. How can I say that with total certainty? Because you are not your own; you were bought with a price, which was paid with the precious blood of Jesus, His beloved Son. He was killed outside the walls of the holy city of Jerusalem so that you could be ushered into the sacred. He took on the stains and guilt of your sin so that you could stand before God blameless and pure. He absorbed all the scorn and contempt of the crowd so that you could hear the voice of the Father calling you redeemed, beloved, chosen.

Grapple with this truth in prayer. Take a moment to meditate on Jesus' suffering. Contemplate the fact that He did that for you. What more could He have done to prove that He is utterly for you?

What are you waiting for? Invite Him in.

If you feel ready, perhaps the words of this prayer can become your own:

Dear Jesus,

I'm afraid to let you come close. I've spent such a long time perfecting the art of protecting myself. I've allowed a wall to build up around my heart, and it's kept me from some hurt, but also from the depth of your love. I know that you desire an intimate relationship with me. And you don't want the fake me.

I would probably keep trying to hustle to prove my worth if I weren't so exhausted. I'd perhaps keep numbing if I weren't so afraid of missing my life. I am so full of baggage and junk, it amazes me that you want me, even when the offering of my heart is tied to self-interest.

How you love me. Because you love me in spite of all of this. You died for me when I was at my worst. I need you, desperately.

I invite you in. I know you purchased my life at a price. I know you chose me. And I choose you. I choose you over self-protection. I choose you over my addictions. I choose you over my other relationships. I choose you over my accomplishments and accolades, my poor attempts to prove my worth.

I want to be utterly "in Christ." Come, Lord Jesus. Here is my heart.

Day Two
ADOPTION

Read Ephesians 1:5–6.

1. What did God destine us for? What was His motive? See Ephesians 1:5.

Adoption denotes receiving all the rights and privileges of those who are born into a family. It means all that Jesus has is ours. This is the source of our true identity. We are adopted daughters of God, who have inherited all the blessings that our hearts and souls need and long for.

2. Read Romans 8:14–17 and describe what it means to be adopted children of God.

Being led by the Holy Spirit is an indicator that we are daughters of God. Does this mean that whenever we aren't led by the Holy Spirit we stop being God's children? No. But it does mean that if we are going to act like who we really are, we are going to seek guidance from the Holy Spirit, and do what He tells us to do. Being "led by the Spirit" may sound a little ethereal and hard to grasp. We don't need to overcomplicate this. What do you sense that God wants you to do right now? There will always be areas where we're confused and unsure, but there is usually some clarity around an area where we'd much prefer to do things our own way. This verse is telling us that a daughter of God recognizes that she is not her own, that she was purchased for a price, and that she should go where God is telling her to go. But as a beloved daughter, she trusts that even if it isn't the plan she prefers, it's ultimately for her benefit.

So how does fear factor into all of this? Why did Saint Paul tell us that we don't have a spirit within us that causes us to fall back into fear? He brings fear up at this point because it's such a powerful emotion, especially when it's unspoken. Silent fear is paralyzing, but spoken fear can propel us forward. Underneath much of what we fear is a sense of losing control. Saint Paul says that we don't need to fall back into fear because he knows who is ultimately in control. He knows that God, in His infinite wisdom, has got all the details straight and is able to bring order and peace. Saint Paul knows that God, in His infinite goodness, is utterly *for us*. As a daughter of God grows in trust of God—in His love for her and His consistent delivery on all His promises—fear starts to lose its grip on her heart. Trust in God is the only true counterweight to fear.

3. As a daughter of God, what can you count on? Read the following verses and record your thoughts.

Matthew 6:31–34

Matthew 10:29–31

Romans 8:38–39

4. You have been destined for adoption through Jesus "in accord with the favor of [God's] will." This has been God's plan all along. For what purpose, according to Ephesians 1:6?

God chooses us for Himself, out of love, and invites us to participate with Him in the epic love story He has been writing throughout history. Each one of us has been created for our own sake—never as an object to be used by God. That being said, God longs for our lives to "praise the glory of his grace." Perhaps this is best understood by describing what it is not. It is not crafting a life so that our own names would be known. It's not living so that we have a platform. It's not insisting that we operate every minute in an area that reflects our particular gifts and abilities. It's certainly not taking credit for good in us that is actually due to God's presence in us. When we are most truly ourselves—when we live most authentically as God's beloved daughters—we crucify our egos and want nothing more than for God's grace to be lifted up and seen. The word *grace* means "unmerited favor." All we have is a gift from Him. Our lives should be a living testimony to the difference that God's grace can make in the life of a woman who knows who and *whose* she is.

Quiet your heart and enjoy His presence. . . . You are home in Him.

"This is and has been the Father's work from the beginning—to bring us into the home of His heart." —George MacDonald

When we are at home in the heart of God, we can rest. We can cease our striving. We're close to Him, and are reminded of His strength, goodness, faithfulness, steadfastness, and ability to bring good from the most wretched circumstances. When we get our eyes off ourselves and on Him, our shoulders can lower a couple of inches as we realize that it isn't up to us. He hasn't asked us to save the world—that was Jesus' job. We aren't strong enough to live the way God wants us to on our own. We see how enormous He is—the immensity of His power and grace. We remember that we are little. And this is a good thing. It leaves more room for God.

We haven't been left alone. Our heavenly Father placed the Holy Spirit in our hearts so that we are able to do the impossible. So that we can be reminded that we belong. So that we never forget how precious we are.

Quiet your heart, and ask the Holy Spirit to fill you. Ask Him to help you to believe that you really are God's beloved daughter. Ask Him to help your mind to be bathed in God's love, so that you see yourself through His eyes.

Day Three
LAVISH GRACE

Read Ephesians 1:7–10.

1. In the original Greek, Ephesians 1:3–14 was actually one long sentence. It's a continuous thought, a prayer praising God. It's as if one amazing blessing after another was parading before Paul's eyes, and he couldn't write fast enough, trying to get it all down on paper. We've already looked at two of those blessings—being chosen and being adopted. What additional blessings are listed in Ephesians 1:7–9?

2. The word *redemption* means "liberation of a slave or a captive by the payment of a ransom." It's buying a slave out of slavery to set her free. This is what Jesus did for you. What was used to pay your ransom? See Ephesians 1:7 and 1 Peter 1:18–19.

I am guessing that when many of you read the words "the blood of Jesus," your eyes glaze over a little or you skim that part. We can write down the right answer without having any idea what it actually means. The reason it's hard for people to understand the significance of it all is because this concept is explained in the Old Testament, and most of us haven't spent much time understanding that part of the Bible. When we have time, we're far more likely to turn to the New Testament and focus on what Jesus said. This is why these words of Saint Paul are confusing. But the background is accessible; you can understand it. It has remained a mystery for most of us because few people have taken the time to summarize it in a way that isn't fifty chapters long and theologically dense. So I've done my best to summarize it in three pages in Appendix 2, "Nothing but the Blood of Jesus," and I'd love it if you would read it now and come back to this section. These words will mean so much more to you if you have this background under your belt.

3. Jesus' blood purchased your freedom. Yet how many of us live out of that reality? Are there areas of your life where you feel enslaved, stuck, or powerless? Are there patterns of sin that you wish you could break away from, but you feel unable to do so? List them here.

What I'm about to share is counterintuitive, yet it is absolutely true. Bear with me and just consider the possibility that believing this can bring the change you are after.

Sometimes the thing we most hate in our lives—whatever it is that makes us feel so powerless—is the very thing God is using to reveal to us that we desperately need Him. What if the starting point for an authentic, personal relationship with Christ is not you strapping on your power pack and proving you are worth something? He meets you most intimately when you let that weight fall to the ground and extend your empty hands. It doesn't make logical sense . . . yet isn't this the desire of our hearts?

Jesus understands how it feels to be powerless. Here is what is amazing: He *chose* to be powerless on the cross. He could have gained control of the situation and called down legions of angels to come to his aid. But instead, He submitted to powerlessness so that you and I could be ransomed.

Jesus chose powerlessness so that you could experience His power in the areas of your life that feel out of control. Look back at your list. All those things you wrote about that make you feel enslaved? He longs for you to be free from each one of them. He wants you to be able to live "in Him" to such a degree that even if your circumstances don't change, something inside *you* does, which allows you to live free, right where you are. This mental shift allows us to rest in the truth that He is in control, even if we are not.

4. Let's move on to the next blessing covered in Ephesians 1:7: forgiveness.

We live in a culture that elevates the importance of protecting self-esteem to an extraordinary level. We want a steady diet of pep talks, encouragement, and someone pointing out our areas of giftedness. No one wants to be reminded that we actually are sinners who need forgiveness. But that's the truth, and until we acknowledge it, we'll never feel the release and freedom that God intends for us.

We have forgiveness of our transgressions on the basis of, or according to, what? See Ephesians 1:7.

Notice what that verse *doesn't* say. It doesn't say we're forgiven because we finally measure up. It doesn't say we're forgiven because truth is relative and sin doesn't matter or exist. It says that payment for our sins is drawn from the riches of God's grace, which is limitless.

God forgives us because He loves us unconditionally. Jesus paid the penalty in our place. The cross is where mercy kisses judgment and both are satisfied.

5. What does Ephesians 1:9–10 say that God has made known to us?

When the word *mystery* is used in Ephesians, it's used to describe God's big rescue plan that was revealed in Jesus after being kept a secret in the past. As we grow in wisdom and insight, we're going to appreciate that plan more and more. This transforming knowledge is available to God's beloved daughters, but we have to pursue it. It's on offer, but if we choose to gorge on social media and Netflix, we'll probably find we're not hungry enough to search for eternal truth, or we're too numbed to allow ourselves to feel the true hunger pangs. The choice is ours.

Quiet your heart and enjoy His presence. . . . You are free in Him.

". . . a plan for the fullness of times, to sum up all things in Christ, in heaven and on earth." (Ephesians 1:10)

God's big plan is to "sum up all things in Christ"—both in heaven and on earth. He knew we would never be able to earn our way into His family, so He sent us an older brother to fight our battles for us. Because of Him, we are ransomed out of slavery and forgiven. We're invited to draw near and learn more about the mysteries of what matters most in life. We can be in Christ, and all He has is ours.

But—we have to recognize who bought our ticket to the party. It was Jesus. He is at the head of our table, so to speak. God's plan is for everything to come under the headship of Christ. He is the one in charge. But this isn't something we need to be afraid of, because He's the kind of host who only wants what is best for us and just waits to lavish us with grace.

It is enormously freeing to realize that someone is in charge, and it's not you or me. Yes, it's a bit of a hit to the ego, but it takes the load off when we recognize that there is a grand plan, and the most benevolent, kind, strong, and steadfast Father is working everything out.

Dear Lord,

I really want to be in control because it makes me feel safe. I like being the one in charge. Until I don't. Until I hit the wall of my limitations and things start to unravel. I don't know why I seem to exhaust every other possibility before I come to you and just lay all my junk at your feet. I literally walk in circles for miles trying to save myself, and it never works. I think it's because I don't fully trust that you are good. Help me to believe in your goodness. Help me to trust. I can't do it on my own.

So I'm coming here with all these areas where I feel enslaved and powerless. These are the situations that I don't like and I can't fix. These are the parts of me that I temporarily enjoy and then am disgusted by. I bring you my ego and my desire for recognition. I bring to you my self-reliance. I bring to you my addiction to people's opinions of me. I bring to you my laziness and preference for mindless distraction over Scripture. I bring to you my faithless, wandering heart.

Will you please take all this mess and forgive me?

Would you please perform a miracle and create something good out of this chaos?

Would you show me what I need to let go of in order to receive your power in this place where I feel powerless?

I am holding out my hands to you in surrender. Distill the nervousness within me and replace it with confident expectation. Remove the fear within me and replace it with trust. Take away the worries and replace them with memories of all the times you have come through for me in the past. I am placing myself at your feet, saying, "I hand my concern over to you. Please take care of everything."

Thank you for lavishing me with the riches of your grace.

Day Four
DESTINY

Read Ephesians 1:11–16.

1. A. Which two words are used to describe us in Ephesians 1:11?

    B. According to verse 11, to what end is God accomplishing all things?

God has had a rescue plan from the very beginning of time. That plan is to ransom us from the exhausting slavery of our own efforts and place us under the tender and safe care of Christ. One day, everything and everyone will be "summed up in Christ," gathered under His banner as we acknowledge Him as our King. Everything that happens in our lives is ordered toward that end. We are chosen and destined to be a part of His grand story.

Do we live like this?

Sometimes. Perhaps on a good day, here and there. But far too many of us are walking around in one of two ways—either with an overwhelming sense of hopelessness or with the crippling burden of responsibility. The hopelessness leads us to wonder what is the point of it all. We can't make sense of the randomness of tragedy and injustice in our world. The confusion that results can cause us to question whether God really is in control, whether He has an overall plan that is ordered to our good. All too often, we conclude that it's really up to us. We have got to pull things together. The result? We carry the weight of the world on our shoulders.

    C. How do you feel when you think of God having an overarching plan? Secure? Controlled? Settled? Lazy?

Sometimes reading about God's plan feels comforting, while other times something in you starts to wonder how free will plays into this. If everything is just moving along toward a predetermined end, why should we bother to pray? Doesn't God already know how it's all going to work out? Does it matter what we do? So hang tight if this subject feels a little messy to you. We're going to circle back to it later.

2. Why is God accomplishing all things according to His will? See Ephesians 1:12.

Here it is, our reason for existence. We exist to bring glory to Him, not ourselves. He is the starting point of everything. If we ever want to be truly satisfied, our primary focus has got to be on God. If we make it all about us, we will miss the point entirely. Our story is set within His larger story. Only as we see that will all the other pieces (the sorrow, the heartache, the struggle to belong and to feel chosen) make sense. We exist for Him, not the other way around. Does this mean we are cogs in a wheel, unimportant as individuals? No. Does it mean that God created us so that we could follow Him around as sycophants, bootlickers, and brownnosers? Again, no.

It means God knows that the only way we are going to be truly fulfilled, whole, and satisfied is if we fix our eyes on Him. If we focus on ourselves, we'll turn into navel-gazers who'll fluctuate between feeling superior and feeling prideful, thus ultimately feeling bad about ourselves and swimming in shame.

When we lose ourselves in Christ, we are found. It's the sure path to safety and significance.

I know that can seem hard to believe. Give it time. Building trust with God can be a gradual process, just like with any other relationship. We have to give Him a chance to reveal Himself to us, and the best way for us to get to know Him is to read the love letter He left behind, which is the Bible. You are doing exactly what you should be doing if you want to grow in trust. Some of the things I'm writing may seem too good to be true. They aren't, I promise you, but it may take a little while for truths to travel from your head to your heart. And that's OK. What's important is to keep journeying forward toward Him.

3. What happens to us when we hear the word of truth and believe in Christ? See Ephesians 1:13.

The Greek word *sphragizó*, translated *seal*, means "to mark a person or thing, to set a mark upon by the impress of a seal, to stamp." In the ancient world, a letter was closed with a wax seal that served to guarantee the identity of the author. It was also used to show ownership; for instance, a cow would be sealed, or branded, with its owner's initials. In this way, the Holy Spirit acts as a seal within us, confirming that we are created by God, that we belong to Him and are under His protection.

4. A. The Holy Spirit is given to us as the first installment or down payment of what?

B. How is that inheritance described in 1 Peter 1:4?

Quiet your heart and enjoy His presence. . . . The "more" that we are after is found here, in Him.

Most of our lives feel messy. Maybe one area is pulled together, but there's always something out of our control. This reality will cause some of us to give up and numb out. Others will push and perform and perfect. Neither response will get us the "more" that we long for.

Remember that in Ephesians 1:10 we are told that God's overall plan is to rescue us and "gather up all things in Jesus." It is only when that happens in our lives, when all our mess is gathered up in Jesus, when we allow Him to be at the helm, that healing and restoration will happen.

What are you running hard after? Peace? Control? Order? Satisfaction? What would change if you ran after Him instead? He is the King you've been waiting for—the only One with the wisdom, power, justice, and compassion needed to heal what is broken in you and in the world.

You have not been left alone to figure this out. You don't need a best friend, a boyfriend, a husband, or a child to complete you and accompany you. You need Jesus. And He promises to be enough. He is more than enough. *Even when it might not feel like He's enough in the moment, our doubt and fear cannot change who He is—our all-sufficient one.*

He left you the Holy Spirit to confirm that He is with you and to give you a taste of the fullness you are going to experience one day in heaven. We receive the Holy Spirit through the sacraments of baptism and confirmation, but if we stop there, as if it's nothing but a box to be checked, we'll never experience the fullness of life that God intended for us.

Perhaps it feels like I'm speaking of a relationship with God that is more intimate than what you have known. The depth to which we're impacted by the sacraments has everything to do with how we have responded in the years after receiving them. We appropriate the power of the Holy Spirit through conversion and prayer. If you want to know more about what conversion is, if you wonder if it's something you have experienced, I encourage you to read Appendix 3, "Conversion of Heart."

When we turn to the Lord (turning is a critical part of conversion), we can see ourselves reflected in His eyes. We see our inherent dignity—our true identity as chosen, destined, beloved daughters of God.

The life God intends for us to live is so much more than going through the motions. It can feel like a wild, unpredictable ride. It will involve suffering. But only as your relationship with Jesus comes together will the rest of your life come together.

Day Five
ENLIGHTENMENT

Read Ephesians 1:17–23.

1. Verse 17 explodes with a big reveal. This is where Paul tells us *why* he has been teaching us all these truths. He prays that we'd be given a spirit of wisdom and revelation for what purpose?

Paul wants us to know who we are (beloved daughters of God) and what we have (blessings, an inheritance, redemption, forgiveness . . .), so that we would know Jesus better and better.

The goal is not for us to become smarter sinners. The goal is not for us to know *about* Jesus. Paul is praying that we would know Jesus *personally*, in such a way that we are increasingly transformed as we grow in intimate knowledge of Him.

As the prayer continues in verses 18 and 19, Paul pleads with God that we would be enlightened to know three things. We'll look at them one by one.

2. A. In Ephesians 1:18, Paul prays that we would know the _____ that belongs to God's call.

The definition of Christian hope is utterly different from the way the word is usually used. Normally when we say, "I hope," we mean "I wish" or "It would be great if . . ." We might say, "I hope the weather is good tomorrow," or "I hope we win the game." Christian hope is much more certain than that. It's a solid belief in what is coming in the future, which totally changes the way you look at your present circumstances. Let me give you an example to illustrate the point.

Say we have two women who are both put in absolutely miserable situations at work. They are going to have to spend a whole day in a room that is cold and smells like dirty socks, alongside a petty coworker who talks constantly, and another who has an annoying habit of humming loudly all day long. The room is a mess, with half-eaten takeout containers all over the place. Add to that a boss who keeps peering over employees' shoulders, criticizing, yelling, and shaming all the while. One woman is told that she is going to be paid fifty dollars for her day of work. The other is told that at the end of the day, she is going to be given a million dollars. Do you not think that the women will look at their current circumstances differently based on what they are hoping for at the end of the day? Don't you think that the one who was promised a million dollars will be able to deal with the irritations and hurts better than the one who was promised fifty dollars? That's what Christian hope can do. When we truly grasp what we have been promised in eternity, we are able to walk through difficulties of this life with an entirely different attitude.

We are not promised that today is going to be easy. In fact, we are assured that we will face trials of many kinds here. But we are promised that one day, in heaven, God will wipe every tear from our eyes. Death will be no more; mourning and crying and pain will be no more (Revelation 21:4).

B. Is there an area of your life where you are lacking hope in the way we have just defined it? Can you list it here, and follow it with a prayer, asking God to help you fix your eyes on all He has promised you in eternity?

3. A. In Ephesians 1:18, Paul prays that we would know the _____ of _____ in his inheritance.

The next thing Paul wants us to know is the "riches of glory in his inheritance." This verse is not talking about *our* inheritance. It's talking about *God's* inheritance.

It says that God's inheritance is among the holy ones. That is referring to *us,* to God's children. This is an utterly unbelievable truth, and if we could only grasp it, we would truly see our worth and value. It means we are God's most precious possession. God looks at everything He owns—the earth and all that's in it, the entire cosmos—then looks at you and says, "She is my inheritance. She is more valuable than everything else in the universe put together. When I point to what matters most, I point to her." We read this again in 1 Peter 2:9: "But you are a chosen people, a royal priesthood, a holy nation, *God's special possession,* that you may declare the praises of him who called you out of darkness into his wonderful light" (emphasis added).

B. What is it like for you to read these verses and hear these words? Can you look at yourself in this light? Can you see that when God looks at you, He feels wealthy? List below all the things you have learned in this lesson about who you are in Christ. Go back and read this again and again. What might happen if you absorbed these truths in your core? What might change? This is who you really are.

4. A. In Ephesians 1:19, Paul prays that we would know the surpassing greatness of His _____.

B. When this same power was "worked in Christ," what occurred? See Ephesians 1:20.

This is one of my favorite passages in the Bible. If we could truly grasp the truth contained here, we would live so differently. The very same power that raised Jesus from the dead is found in the hearts of God's daughters. This flies in the face of our sense of powerlessness. This is God's response when we say, "I can't." God never towers over us in our weakness and tells us to pull ourselves up by our bootstraps. He crouches low, He comes down, in order to tenderly remind us that what we can't do by ourselves, *His* power can do within us—in spite of us.

C. Where do you need His power in your life? List it here, then write out 1 John 4:4 beneath those words. Follow it with a short prayer, asking God for the grace to see what most people don't see—the divine power hidden within your soul. Ask Him to help you live out that reality.

I need to experience God's power in this area of my life:

1 John 4:4

Dear Lord,

Quiet your heart and enjoy His presence. . . . There is fullness in Him.

"[His power is] far above every principality, authority, power, and dominion, and every name that is named not only in this age but also in the one to come. And he put all things beneath his feet and gave him as head over all things to the church, which is his body, the fullness of the one who fills all things in every way." (Ephesians 1:21–23)

When you feel powerless, what do you usually do to reestablish a sense of security and control? Maybe you determine to perfect your performance. Some of us obsess about what we eat and try to maintain the illusion of control in that way. A lot of the time we look at the people around us and place the blame on their shoulders. When we're overwhelmed by our lack of resources, when the voice that says we are not enough is loud enough, many of us just check out.

Jesus offers us a different choice. He asks us to switch our focus from our powerlessness to His power. Whatever we think gives power—wealth, prestige, intelligence, influence, gender, race—He is more. There is no authority, name, or position that is higher than Christ the King. He is the only One who can fill us with what we need.

Yes, you face situations that seem insurmountable. Yes, you might currently be in a situation that feels hopeless. Yes, your problems are weighty. Yes, the ache in your heart is profound. Yes, the dreams you have buried can cause you to feel you can't go on. All of it is real.

But the power that is lodged, anchored, firmly fixed in the core of your being comes straight from an unlimited source—God Himself. That power is just as real as the obstacles you face, and it is greater. *You can overcome. The beginning of your story does not need to determine how it ends. Grasp hold of your Deliverer. Ask Him to pour out His immeasurable power on your behalf.*

Conclusion

"It is Jesus you seek when you dream of happiness; he is waiting for you when nothing else you find satisfies you; he is the beauty to which you are so attracted; it is he who provokes you with that thirst for fullness that will not let you settle for compromise; it is he who urges you to shed the masks of a false life." —*Saint John Paul II*

It is Jesus who calls you to freedom, inviting you to step into your true identity. You are beloved. You are forgiven. The slate is wiped clean. You are a precious child of God. He wants the chains that keep you tied to the opinions of others, the sins of your past, and the condemnation and shame you feel to be broken. And He has the power to break them.

You are no longer a slave to fear and hopelessness. You are precious and you are free. You are worthy and you are strong. You are never alone—you are surrounded by the arms of the Father and He is faithful and true.

He is calling your name, right now. He is asking you to step out into the unknown—into a totally new way of living. He is asking you to begin the journey of growing in your trust of His perfect love. He is offering you a rescue.

A warning: This journey to all He's promised doesn't take you *around* the Red Sea; it takes you *through* it. It's a path with walls of water on either side. You can choose what you're going to dwell on. You can stare at the water, just waiting for it to crash, or you can keep your eyes fixed on Jesus and on the fact that He is keeping the ground dry just in front of you. It's dry enough for one step. There is grace for one more day. So hold on. Grasp hold of hope. Dig deep in your soul and reach for His power. Keep your eyes on Jesus to avoid navel-gazing and losing sight of your Savior. Ask for eyes of love that begin to recognize God's presence, which has been there all along. You are chosen.

My Resolution

"My Resolution" is your opportunity to write down one specific, personal application from this lesson. We can take in a lot of information from studying the Bible, but if we don't translate it into action, we have totally missed the point. In James 1:22, we're told that we shouldn't just hear the Word of God; we are to "do what it says." So what qualities should be found in a good resolution? It should be **personal** (use the pronouns *I, me, my, mine*), it should be **possible** (don't choose something so far-fetched that you'll just become discouraged), it should be **measurable** (a specific goal to achieve within a specific time period), and it should be **action oriented** (not just a spiritual thought).

Examples:

1. I will write out a description of my true identity in Christ on an index card. I will carry it with me and read it throughout the day.

2. When I start to feel like I am hustling to prove my worth (clues: my stomach is upset; my heart is racing; I'm getting snippy with people around me), I will consider this a red flag inviting me to stop and look at my motives. What am I trying to prove? I will remember that in Christ, I can rest. I can trust Him with the results. It is not all up to me.

3. I will go to confession this week because I long to be showered in mercy. I cling to the truth that when I approach God in humility, I am never met with condemnation. He forgives, always. I claim the promise that when I am forgiven, God removes the sin from me as far as east is from the west (Psalm 103:12).

My resolution:

 NOTES

Lesson 3

CHOSEN TALK

Accompanying talk can be viewed by DVD or digital download purchase or access online at walkingwithpurpose.com/videos.

I. Wake Up to the Battle

You've got to KNOW the truth and PROTECT the truth.
You've got to RECOGNIZE your identity and OWN your identity.
You've got to BELIEVE the gospel and PREACH it to yourself every day.

II. Examine Your Own Life

Dr. Bob Schachts' research on wounds and identity lies:

WOUNDS	HOW THEY DISTORT OUR IDENTITY
Abandonment	"I am all alone. No one understands me."
Shame	"I am bad, dirty, perverted . . . it's my fault."
Fear	"If I trust, speak, confront, I will be hurt or die."
Powerlessness	"I feel overwhelmed . . . I don't know what to do."
Rejection	"I am not loved or wanted . . . I have no value."
Hopelessness	"It's never going to change . . . there is no hope."
Confusion	"I don't know what is happening to me."[1]

These wounds are real. Our stories—the circumstances that led us to believe lies about our identity—they have shaped us.

---

[1] Bob Schuchts, *Be Healed* (Notre Dame, IN: Ave Maria Press, 2014), 115.

III. God is the Author of Your Story

Why are we here? What is the purpose of our lives?
Ephesians 1:12

"I saw His glory in my wounds and it dazzled me." Saint Augustine[2]

This is what we will want to be able to say when we meet God:

> In my weakness, I knew You to be strong.
> In my wounds, I saw You as my healer.
> In my need, I saw Your all-sufficiency.
> In my sin, I knew You to be my Savior.
> In my despair, You were my hope.
> In my rejection, I was Your beloved.
> In my abandonment, You were there.
> In my confusion, You were wisdom.
> In my fear, You were courage.
> In my shame, You covered me.
> In my powerlessness, You ransomed me.
> In my hopelessness, You resurrected me.

Discussion Questions

1. What counterfeit identities do many of us unknowingly take on-board? Which one do you believe is a part of your story? (Some examples: the fixer, the mistake, the achiever, the scapegoat, the one who gets things done, the unloved, the good one, the lost one.)

2. Share a story of a time God brought something good out of intense personal suffering, creating meaning out of suffering that felt wasted previously. This could be from your own life or from a life observed. Speak as personally as possible.

3. What would change in your life if you lived daily with your perspective set on eternity?

---

[2] Melanie Jean Juneau, "Find Christ's Joy In Your Deepest Wounds," Catholic365.com, http://www.catholic35.com/article/5775/find-christs-joy-in-your-deepest-wounds.html, accessed October 30, 2017.

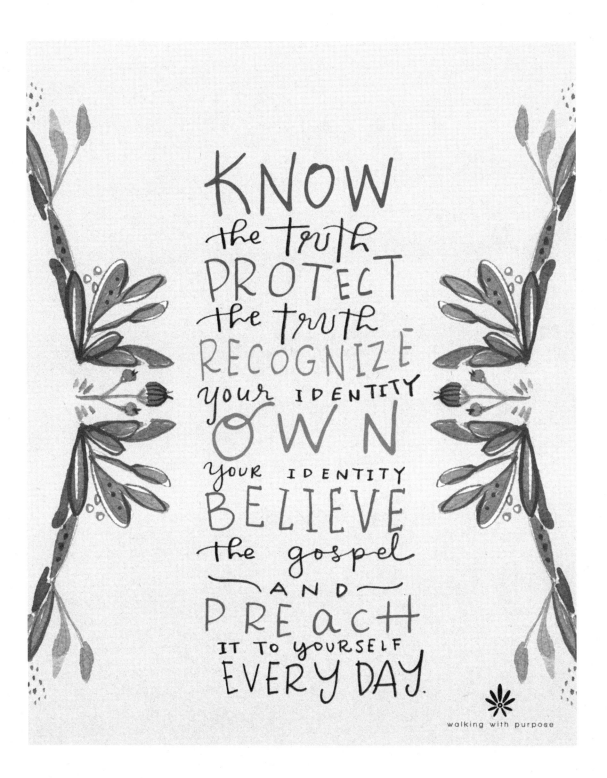

KNOW
the truth
PROTECT
the truth
RECOGNIZE
your IDENTITY
OWN
your IDENTITY
BELIEVE
the gospel
AND
PREACH
IT TO YOURSELF
EVERY DAY.

walking with purpose

# NOTES

Lesson 4

GROUNDED BIBLE STUDY

Introduction

I forced myself to watch a movie last night—not because I was feeling tempted to overwork, as in needing to force myself to rest, but because the subject matter of the film was so upsetting that I wanted to cover my eyes and turn away. The movie, *12 Years a Slave*, tells the story of a free-born African American man who is kidnapped in Washington, D.C., and sold into slavery in the deep South of 1841. Immersing myself in the cruelty and suffering of that time was sobering and vexing, especially because I know man's propensity to sink to that level remains the same today as it was two hundred years ago. My thoughts scan the globe, and the horrific amount of sex trafficking that goes on today grieves me to my core. With these images of abuse and wickedness still running through my mind, my heart is screaming out for justice—for an end to the evil.

And then a quote from Aleksandr Solzhenitsyn comes to mind: "If only it were all so simple! If only there were evil people somewhere insidiously committing evil deeds, and it were necessary only to separate them from the rest of us and destroy them. But the line dividing good and evil cuts through the heart of every human being. And who is willing to destroy a piece of his own heart?"[3]

The problem lies within our own hearts, as well as outside us. This is a sobering truth that makes us reach for something distracting or numbing. Please resist this temptation. Leaning in at this point will fill in some blanks for you that you have been wanting to see addressed. You may not be outright asking for it, but we all have had an underlying sense that something is not right. That is actually the gift of guilt. Guilt gets a lot of bad press in our current culture, but believe me, once it is gone we are in serious trouble. Guilt alerts us to the existence of something that needs to be looked at and repaired. No one likes going through a painful test looking for cancer (a

---

[3] Aleksandr Solzhenitsyn, *The Gulag Archipelago 1918–1956* (Boulder, CO: Westview Press, 1998), 168.

mammogram comes to mind), but we'd like circumstances far less if we had no way to be alerted to something that would kill us if we didn't seek a remedy.

I am known in my family for having no sense of direction whatsoever. Recently, I was enjoying my route home from the airport, thanking God for the beauty of the fields and horses that I was passing by. My prayer went something like this: "Thank you, God, for this pure unexpected delight! I've never noticed these farms before. It is so good to finally be slowing down and actually seeing things I never noticed the countless other times I drove on this road." My quiet reverie ended when I saw a sign for a town that I knew was nowhere near my destination. It didn't matter how many other people were on the road with me, or that everything seemed fine. No matter how much I had been enjoying the road, no matter how confident I'd been in the route I'd chosen, no matter how many other cars were headed in the same direction, I was on the fast track to nowhere.

It's a gift when someone points out that we are heading in the wrong direction, and that's where Paul begins in Ephesians 2. We don't need one more person telling us that everything is just fine and we should be grateful. Something *is* wrong, and unless we own our part of it, we'll never find the relief we are searching for.

Day One
GROUNDED IN REALITY

Gear up for today's reading. These verses do not massage your soul with sweetness. This is like the needle going in for a blood test. It isn't going to kill you, but it isn't going to be very pleasant.

Read these verses in light of our previous lessons. Remember who you are in Christ. The truths of Ephesians 2:1–3 are not intended to lead you to shame. God allows the Holy Spirit to convict us. We experience this as guilt, and it alerts us that something needs to change. The enemy prefers to use shame, because it causes us to feel condemned and hopeless. Guilt convicts our souls of the effects of our sin, but shame tells us we are bad. And this is precisely the moment we most need Jesus. Let's pray before we dive in.

Dear Jesus,

Thank you for promising me in Romans 10:11 that "everyone that believes in [you] will not be put to shame." Protect me from the paralyzing power of shame. Help me to resist the urge to hide and cover up. Give me strength to look within, knowing that even as I open my eyes to sin in my life, you are right there, offering forgiveness and grace, always and without fail. May your voice calling me beloved be louder than any voice that calls me damaged beyond repair. Protect me from self-contempt. Clothe my nakedness and vulnerability with your garment of grace. Amen.

Read Ephesians 2:1–3.

1. Ephesians 2:1 describes our state of being when we are apart from Christ. What did Saint Paul say we are like before we encounter Jesus?

The word translated *sins* is *hamartia,* a word used to describe shooting. It's a description of missing the mark—of failing to be who we could and should be. *Transgressions* comes from the word *paraptoma,* which means "to slip or fall." It's a falling off of the ideal path, a straying. Without Jesus, this is the state of affairs.

Saint Paul lets us know that we aren't just stuck in that place; we are actually dead there—utterly helpless and unable to move. This is what sin does. It kills us. First, it destroys our innocence. Then it attacks and decimates our will to live differently, because each sin makes the next one easier. Ultimately, our will can become so dead that we are enslaved to the sin, utterly mastered by it.

2. A. Ephesians 2:2–3 identifies three forces at work encouraging us to stay in that place of slavery and death. What are they?

These are the forces that encourage us to go in the wrong direction. Some Bibles replace the phrase "age of this world" with "the spirit of the age." This is the pull of our culture—one that values consumerism, individualism, superficiality, immediate gratification, power, prestige, lust, and comfort.

B. The ruler of the power of the air is the devil. How is the devil described in CCC 2851? (The Catechism Clips can be found at the end of this lesson.)

C. The third force is "the desires of our flesh." This isn't just referring to sins that relate to our bodies; it's also referring to the disorder we experience in our minds and hearts. Read Galatians 5:19–21 and list what Saint Paul meant by "the desires of the flesh."

Unpacking these three forces explains why it's so hard to stay on the right path. There is a lot working against our best intentions to be whole and free. The good news of Ephesians 2 is coming, but before we get there, we need to dive a little deeper into what is at the root of our trouble.

When we go in the same direction as the majority of people, when we live the way the present age lives, self is always at the center. Human nature, left to its own devices, is profoundly selfish. It's a constant calculation of how current circumstances and people can best benefit you.

We can all think of extreme examples of this in history: the tyrants who practiced genocide and slavery; those who used and abused power. Their self-absorption is easy to identify. Some of us don't have to look outside our own family or childhood to see someone who used and abused power.

What we are slower to recognize is how often this self-centeredness manifests in moral and religious people. In the quest to satisfy the ego, most people go in another direction. Nothing feels better than being really good. Checking the religious boxes, serving the poor, rocking it as a mom or a daughter or an employee or a boss . . . all these things make life feel more meaningful. But whom are we doing this for? That's the key question. Our motive matters. Are we doing it because it makes us feel better, in which case it's ultimately about us? Or is it about and for God?

How do we identify what our motives really are? One way is to check how we react when God doesn't give us our way. When we pray for something and God doesn't give it to us, does it make us angry? Do we cry foul? Do we point to all the good things we've done and ask Him why He is ignoring us? Do we tell Him that this isn't fair? If so, it's quite possible that we have been behaving in order to get what we want from God. This isn't loving Him; this is using Him, and at the heart of it is self-centeredness.

3. A. Can you recognize self-centeredness in yourself? In which areas of your life or which relationships? Can you identify any relationships in which you are using people instead of serving them? Has this ever been the case in your relationship with God?

   B. Do you long to be set free from egotism and self-absorption? What are you willing to give up in order to experience this? Is freedom in this area worth more to you than power, prestige, or comfort?

4. A. I realize that this can all be a little confusing. If you are a Christian, you may be wondering why you can recognize yourself in this description of life without Christ. The key to making sense of this is found in verse 3, hidden in a better understanding of what is meant by the "wishes of the flesh and the impulses." The word *wishes* can also be translated *concupiscence*. Read the definition of *concupiscence* found at the end of this lesson in the Catechism Clips and record it here.

   B. Read CCC 1426 and answer the following questions:

   i. What has made us holy and without blemish?

   ii. What did "the new life received in Christian initiation" *not* abolish? What did it *not* get rid of within us?

iii. What is the struggle of conversion directed toward?

This means that even when we've experienced conversion of heart, even when we know and follow Jesus, it's going to be a struggle to do the right thing. We are no longer dead in our sins, but we are going to still feel the pull of the forces that tempt us to go in the wrong direction.

Quiet your heart and enjoy His presence. . . . Come into the warmth of His embrace.

Ephesians 2:3 says that "we were by nature children of wrath." As you read that verse, it may strike you as being at odds with the image (and truth) that you are a beloved daughter of God. It helps to take a look at Romans 1. In this chapter of the Bible, Saint Paul wrote about how the wrath of God is a picture of Him giving us over to our sin, allowing us to experience the consequences of our choices. God does not do this because He delights in seeing us reap what we've sown. His hope is that when we taste the consequences of our actions, we'll come to our senses like the Prodigal Son and turn back to Him.

Because of original sin, we are all born outside the covenant of grace. Through baptism, we come back into the embrace of God the Father, Jesus, and the Holy Spirit. God wants us to stay close to Him, encircled by His love, care, and protection. When we step out of the embrace, it is always by our own choice. We leave; He woos us back. His preference would be for us to learn the easy way—to just trust Him when He tells us what sinful choices will result in. But all too often, we end up learning the hard way.

Although we will continue to feel the pull of forces that urge us to choose comfort and selfishness, we are not helpless and dead. As we learned in Ephesians 1:19, the same power that raised Jesus from the dead dwells inside us and gives us all we need to choose to go in the right direction. Jesus didn't come to make bad women better. He came to make dead women fully alive again.

Are you ready to turn? Do you long for the power of shame to be broken in your life? Turn to Jesus. Come fragile. Come fractured. Come with your brokenness, and ask Him to be your gentle healer. He will not refuse you. Come back to the embrace of your Creator, Redeemer, and Sanctifier.

Day Two
GROUNDED IN GRACE

Read Ephesians 2:4–10.

After spending Day One looking at what it means to be dead in our sins, hope rushes at us with the first two words of Ephesians 2:4: *But God.* We were dead, we followed the wishes of the flesh, we were children of wrath . . . *but God* is rich in mercy, and that changes everything. He rescues us and sets us on a completely different path.

1. A. How is our past state described in the first part of Ephesians 2:5?

    B. But when God intervened, what happened? See Ephesians 2:5–6.

    C. How are we spiritually made alive? See John 5:24, Romans 6:4, and CCC 1213.

Our baptism isn't just a rite of passage that gives us an excuse for a party. It's the ultimate spiritual wakening as we move from death to life. We are made just and receive the Divine indwelling at Baptism. It's a significant moment in our lives when God publicly declares our true identity and how loved we are. Through this sacrament, we go from being estranged from God to being enfolded in His arms and welcomed into our heavenly family. We are united with Jesus, and the blessing that God spoke over Him at His baptism is spoken over us: "This is my daughter, the beloved, with whom I am well pleased." Dr. Bob Schuchts describes it this way:

> Baptism is one of God's primary weapons against the tactics of our adversary. It is an infusion of God's love into our hearts and an objective marker that proclaims we have been sealed as the Father's beloved. Always remember you are the beloved child in whom your Father delights; you are marked and sealed in the name of the living God, who now lives inside you.[4]

---

[4] Bob Schuchts, *Be Transformed: The Healing Power of the Sacraments* (Notre Dame, IN: Ave Maria Press), 47.

CCC 1213 tells us that baptism is the gateway to life in the Spirit. This is huge when it comes to our identity, because it's the Holy Spirit within us who reminds us that we are daughters of God (Romans 8:16).

You may be reading this and thinking to yourself, "I've been baptized, so why haven't I experienced this? Why don't I *feel* like I'm God's beloved child?" It may be that you have had experiences of rejection in your life that make it hard to believe that God truly loves you as a precious daughter. Voices of people who didn't love you well may be crowding out the gentle voice of the Holy Spirit calling you beloved. Perhaps the love you have encountered has been conditional and hard to count on. It helps to remember that God's fatherly love is based on something entirely separate from your behavior. It's based on something that will never change, shift, or be taken away. It's based on what Jesus has done, not on anything you can do. It's a free gift of grace, not something earned through your performance.

2. A. According to Ephesians 2:5–9, how are we saved?

A critical part of the Wakening is realizing what saves us. It isn't our good works. It isn't our perfection. It isn't the hustle. It's grace at work in our souls.

B. How is grace defined in CCC 1996 and CCC 1999?

3. Read the following commentary from William Barclay to gain insight into what has made it possible for us to have this incredible Father/daughter relationship with God.

> God is love; sin is therefore a crime, not against law, but against love. Now it is possible to make atonement for a broken law, but it is impossible to make atonement for a broken heart; and sin is not so much breaking God's law as it is breaking God's heart.[5] Let us take a crude and imperfect analogy. Suppose a motorist by careless driving kills a child. He is arrested,

---

[5] Note: God's law is love– it is not legalistic. See CCC 2055 for further study.

tried, found guilty, sentenced to a term of imprisonment and/or to a fine. After he has paid the fine and served the imprisonment, as far as the law is concerned, the whole matter is over. But it is very different in relation to the mother whose child he killed. He can never put things right with her by serving a term of imprisonment and paying a fine. The only thing which can restore his relationship to her is an act of free forgiveness on her part. That is the way we are to God. It is not God's laws against which we have sinned; it is against his heart. And therefore only an act of free forgiveness of the grace of God can put us back into the right relationship with him.[6]

What do you believe is the right response to this gift of mercy, forgiveness, and grace? Do you agree with Barclay's statement that sin is not so much about breaking God's law as it is about breaking His heart?

How do we respond to this unearned gift of grace? We look at the way in which we are living. We determine to stop breaking God's heart with our ungodly self-reliance and self-focus. We respond with obedience, but not because it earns us His favor. We obey God because we know this is the best way to express our love for Him. We obey out of gratitude, not fear, with the awareness that we will never be able to be good enough to earn it. And therein lies the beauty in our brokenness.

This is where faith comes into play. CCC 1993 tells us that grace and man's freedom cooperate together. God first touches our hearts through the Holy Spirit and draws us to Him. He offers us mercy, forgiveness, and shelter. But we have a choice how we'll respond. He won't force Himself on us; He is a gentleman through and through.

It's up to us to choose to exercise the muscle of faith. True faith is much more than just intellectually agreeing with something. It requires a personal commitment that is seen in what we believe, trust, and obey. Just like exercising a muscle, faith isn't exercised once and then ignored afterward. Our faith will grow stronger as we believe moment by moment in God's goodness and grace, trust in His presence and plan, and obey what He has asked of us. It's a matter of entrusting the past, present, and future into the hands of the lover of our souls, who is utterly *for us*.

---

6 William Barclay, *The Letters to the Galatians and Ephesians* (Philadelphia: Westminster Press, 1976), 104–05.

4. How are we described in Ephesians 2:10? What does this verse say that we were created for? Is this how you see yourself?

Quiet your heart and enjoy His presence. . . . His grace has saved you.

You are God's masterpiece—His handcrafted, one-of-a-kind work of art. When He created you, He placed a mission—a purpose—within your heart. You were created to step out into our broken world and do good works—not to earn God's favor or to create a platform for yourself, but to partner with the One who made you to bring restoration to broken places. This is true for every single one of God's daughters. This means that no matter how you currently see yourself, He did not skip you. The more you are living out of your true identity as a beloved daughter, the more you will be able to discover and walk in your true purpose. The enemy of your soul will do all he can to keep you from living this way, but you can catch him in the act of sowing seeds of doubt and condemnation and reject those thoughts.

Spend some time in prayer asking God to help you separate condemnation from conviction. The truth is, we have done things that have broken God's heart. The Holy Spirit convicts us of those sins and calls us to confess them. But if there is something plaguing you that you have already confessed, be assured that this weight of condemnation is not coming from the Holy Spirit. We can hold on to the promise that "There is no condemnation for those who are in Christ Jesus" (Romans 8:1). Be assured, our Father always, always, always keeps His promises.

Dear Lord,

I really struggle to see myself the way you see me. My awareness of my shortcomings and past mistakes can paralyze me in a sea of shame and hopelessness. I often feel like I will never change. Lift me out of these waters. Help me to confess sin quickly and then grab hold of your promises of mercy:

If I confess my sins, you are faithful and just and will forgive them and cleanse me from every wrongdoing (1 John 1:9).

You have removed my sins as far from me as the east is from the west (Psalm 103:12).

Though my sins are like scarlet, you will make them as white as snow. Though they are red like crimson, you will make them as white as wool (Isaiah 1:18).

You have saved me, not because of the righteous things I have done, but because of your mercy. You have washed away my sins, giving me a new birth and new life through the Holy Spirit (Titus 3:5).

Forgive me for the times I don't forgive myself. Help me to understand that when I don't forgive myself for things that you have said are wiped from the record—forgiven and cleansed—I am holding my own standard ds above yours. There is no authority higher than you, so if you say I am forgiven, then it is so. Please grant me freedom and healing in this area of my heart.

You are good. You are steadfast. You are full of grace and mercy. May I lean into all that you are, and find my true identity there, in the depths of your heart.

Day Three
GROUNDED IN BELONGING

Read Ephesians 2:11–22.

This passage is talking about the alienation and separation that existed between the Jewish people and Gentiles (everyone who wasn't Jewish) before Jesus came. To say that there was division between the two groups is something of an understatement. In fact, if a Jew married a Gentile, a funeral for that Jew was given.[7] It was unlawful for a Jew to help a Gentile woman give birth, because that was bringing another Gentile into the world.[8] The Jewish temple, the sacred place of worship, had an actual wall that divided the area where Jewish people were allowed and where the Gentiles could be. Archaeologists have found one of the signs that hung on that wall at the temple, and it says, "No man of another race is to enter within the fence and enclosure around the Temple. Whoever is caught will only have himself to thank for the death which follows."[9]

1. A. Describe the state of the Gentiles without Christ. See Ephesians 2:12.

    B. What happened to the Gentiles because of Jesus? See Ephesians 2:13.

---

[7] Barclay, *Letters to the Galatians and Ephesians*, 107.
[8] Ibid.
[9] Andrew T. Lincoln, *Word Biblical Commentary: Ephesians* (Waco, TX: Word, 1990), 141.

2. Have you ever felt like an outsider? Do you often feel alone or unprotected? Do you ever think no one understands you? Do you feel like you are living on the fringe? If so, describe when you have experienced this. I encourage you to describe the *feeling* more than the logistical details.

3. A. How is Jesus described in Ephesians 2:14? What did He do for outsiders, according to Ephesians 2:14–18?

Just like the Gentiles, we all know what it is like to feel alienated, on the outside looking in. Why do some of us still feel alone and abandoned when the dividing wall has been broken down and we've been invited to draw near? This is an example of a truth from the Bible that we can know and believe intellectually, yet not feel we are experiencing on a day-to-day basis.

Jesus recognizes that sometimes we need some healing on the soul level before we can truly receive truth like this into our hearts. In those times when we have felt like outsiders—rejected, abandoned, or excluded—in those moments when we have been deeply hurt, we are especially susceptible to the lies of the enemy of our soul. We are vulnerable when we're in pain. The enemy knows this, and so he whispers lies about our identity, causing us to question whether we are truly God's beloved daughters. His absolute favorite lies are those that are tied to our identity, because he knows that if he can mess with us here, he is messing with us at the core of who we are. He fights dirty.

People love imperfectly. We know that and expect it to some degree. But unless we totally close off our hearts, we can still get sideswiped. When this happens, we can believe lies like these: I am all alone. No one understands me. No one will ever really love me if they see the real me. It's all up to me; no one will step in to protect me.

These are lies, but in the moment of pain, they sound oh so true. We agree with them because that is how we are feeling in that moment. And because God didn't step in and prevent the hurtful experience from happening, our relationship with Him starts to feel messy as well. Often when that happens, we begin to wrestle with one of two questions: Is God actually good? Can I trust Him? Without us even realizing it, the lies can slide over and start infecting our view of God.

B. Has this been your experience? Have your feelings of abandonment or rejection ever caused you to wonder where God was in your time of suffering? Have you struggled to believe that God really understands you or is there for you?

God wants to come to those places of hurt in our hearts and bring restoration. This is what He promised in Isaiah 57:19: "Peace, peace to the far and the near, says the Lord; and I will heal them." We'll begin exploring how He does this in this session's talk. For now, would you consider asking yourself how open or closed off your heart is to Jesus in His efforts to move toward you in your hurt and fear?

4. No matter how much you might feel like you don't, *you belong*. Write out Ephesians 2:19–22, substituting the first-person pronoun *I* for *you*. This is truth you can stand on. No matter who has rejected you or walked away from you, you belong to God.

Quiet your heart and enjoy His presence. . . . You are no longer far off; He's drawing you close.

In Ephesians 2:14, Jesus is described as our peace. When the Jewish people used the word peace, *it had a broader meaning, encompassing the connotations of the Hebrew word* shalom. *It indicated wholeness, well-being, fullness of blessing.*[10]

Jesus wants to be our peace in such a way that we become fully alive. He wants us to experience the Wakening in such a way that we see the dividing walls going down as we are ushered into a spiritual family that welcomes us home. We are no longer wanderers with nowhere to belong. We have a heavenly Father who adores us, a big brother who will protect us, and a heavenly mother who understands us completely and fights on our behalf as she intercedes for us in prayer.

---

[10] Peter S. Williamson, *Catholic Commentary on Sacred Scripture: Ephesians* (Grand Rapids, MI: Baker Academic, 2009), 71.

We are never alone. Because of this, we do not need to be afraid. We can take courage as we trust in Jesus' words to us in John 14:27: "Peace I leave with you; my peace I give to you. Not as the world gives do I give it to you. Do not let your hearts be troubled or afraid."

Dear Lord,

I long to experience the wholeness, well-being, and fullness of blessing that your peace brings. Instead of numbing or self-protecting because of fear of getting hurt again, I pray I would remember and truly believe that I am never alone and am totally understood by you.

You promised me in Ephesians 2:22 that I am "being built together into a dwelling place of God in the Spirit." A king dwells in the same country as his people. A father dwells in the same house as his children. You come as the lover of my soul and dwell within my heart. You desire this level of intimacy with me so that no matter what circumstances might be swirling around me, in my core, I am steady and fearless because you are there.

Help me shift my focus from what is outside me to what is within me. When I try to satisfy my need for belonging and understanding outside myself, I feel insecure. This is because people, even the best of them, love imperfectly and inconsistently. I ask you to meet my genuine need for a place to belong. May I find my true home in you. What is home? Home is where things are arranged the way that feels comforting and right. Home is where things are set up the way I desire them to be. As I make my home in you, I am comforted and my desires are transformed. I begin to want what you want, and as those desires are purified to match your perfect plan for me, I become fully alive—full of joy and peace. I ask this of you, knowing that you are a good, good Father and that you never hold out on me. You are for me. Utterly. Without fail. Steadfast and sure.

Day Four
GROUNDED IN HOPE

Read Ephesians 3:1–13.

In this passage, Saint Paul interrupts the flow of his letter and digresses. Verses 2–13 are one long parenthesis. It's as if a thought has popped into Paul's head and he needs to talk to us about it before he can continue with his previous point.

It's the phrase "prisoner of Christ" that has sent his thoughts off in a new direction. Paul was imprisoned when he wrote Ephesians, and he knew that his imprisonment was causing anxiety and distress in the hearts of his readers. He wasn't just a teacher—he was a pastor, and he understood the way suffering can shake our faith. As we all know, it doesn't just affect the person walking through the trial; those who care about the person are deeply affected, too. It has been said that the hardest suffering is that which seems senseless. And we are even more baffled when the suffering comes to someone who has loved and obeyed God. When it really is acute, we can so easily become bitter or numb ourselves in an attempt to minimize the pain. We just don't know what else to do with our feelings. Paul knew all of this, and endeavored in this passage to awaken us to a different, higher perspective. These words are his attempt to lift our focus up, in order to keep us from losing heart during our suffering.

1. A. According to Ephesians 3:3–4, what was made known to Paul?

We tend to think of mystery as a genre of book or film in which it's up to us to try to figure out what's going to happen next. When the word *mystery* is used in the Bible, it isn't talking about something that *we* have to uncover; it's something that is *revealed*. God knows the meaning of all mysteries and He chooses to disclose them in His perfect timing. He reveals each mystery because it's not something that we could figure out through the process of reasoning. Revealed mysteries are too profound for us to grasp with our unaided intellects.

B. While God's mystery remained hidden throughout the Old Testament, what has changed since Christ came? See Ephesians 1:9 and 3:9.

C. What is the mystery that has been revealed? See Ephesians 3:6

The gospel of grace is the great mystery that has been revealed. The gospel is radically different from following a set of rules and checking boxes in order to be accepted by God. That sort of system would not need to be revealed to us; we could figure it out quite easily on our own. It makes sense. It seems fair. But a gospel of grace that says our salvation depends on Christ's righteousness, not our own? That says we are all in equal need of forgiveness? That says God draws near to us when we are least deserving? It breaks down our self-righteousness and logical calculations, leaving us speechless with wonder. At least it should.

2. What mission was given to Saint Paul? See Ephesians 3:8–9.

3. A. As Paul brings light to what God's plan has been from the very beginning, "the manifold wisdom of God [is] made known" (Ephesians 3:10). Through whom and to whom is it made known? See Ephesians 3:10.

   B. Verse 11 talks about the eternal purposes that God accomplished through Jesus. We touched on this when we studied Ephesians 1. Going back to that chapter, what has been God's eternal purpose from the very beginning? See Ephesians 1:9–10.

Here's the application: God sees all the brokenness that surrounds us. The disease that ravages our bodies, the divorce and division that devastates our relationships, the death that leaves us overwhelmed with grief . . . He sees it all. He has always known what free will and sin would result in. So He set His plan in motion to sum up all things in Christ, to put all the brokenness back together. God is doing that healing work today, and one day He will bring it to completion.

He makes this known through the Church, specifically through community. This is where Christ is restoring and reconciling, through healed relationships—by breaking down first the walls that divide us from God, and then those that divide us from each other. He is still at work within our communities, giving us the strength and grace to forgive and seek reconciliation. *This* is how the gospel is made known. When people see healing happen in our relationships—when they see different races come together as a Church family, relatives reconcile despite decades of hurt, and spouses offer forgiveness in the face of unfaithfulness—they scratch their heads and look a little closer. They want to know why it's possible. How can suffering end in reconciliation? And this allows us to point to Jesus.

4. What did Paul ask of his readers in Ephesians 3:13?

I acknowledge the complexity of this idea, the weight of it all. As we wrestle with these thoughts, may it call us to prayer.

Quiet your heart and enjoy His presence. . . . His suffering ended in glory.

Paul was always able to keep his suffering in perspective because he fixed his eyes on the big picture: God's plan of salvation. He trusted that the major pieces of that plan and all the minor details were in His hands. This allowed him to believe that no suffering was senseless, and that even if he didn't have answers or clarity to his question of why, God was working everything out to a good end.

This was Paul's radical perspective on being imprisoned: He didn't actually think of himself as held captive by those who put him in chains. The way he describes himself throughout his letters in the New Testament makes it clear that he considered himself a prisoner of Jesus. He referred to himself as a slave of Christ (Romans 1:1, Galatians 1:10), and "taken possession of by Christ" (Philippians 3:12). He would be kept physically in chains only if Jesus permitted it. Christ was the one who was really in charge.

A modern-day example of this comes from the life of a Romanian pastor, Josef Tson. When he was arrested for his faith and then threatened with death, he said the following to his interrogator:

> *What is taking place here is not an encounter between you and me. This is an encounter between my God and me. . . . My God is teaching me a lesson [through you]. I do not know what it is. Maybe He wants to teach me several lessons. I only know, sirs, that you will do to me only what God wants you to do and you will not go one inch further—because you are only an instrument of my Lord. . . . Sir, let me explain how I see this issue. Your supreme weapon is killing. My supreme weapon is dying. Here is how it works. You know that my sermons on tape have spread all over the country. If you kill me, those sermons will be sprinkled with my blood. Everyone will know I died for my preaching. And everyone who has a tape will pick it up and say, "I'd better listen again to what this man preached, because he really meant it; he sealed it with his life." So, sir, my sermons will speak ten times louder than before. I will actually rejoice in this supreme victory if you kill me.[11]*

What a radical perspective on suffering. Can you ask the Lord to widen your perspective so that His eternal plan, not just your suffering, is in view? Can you ask Him for the courage to remain steadfast? Can you ask Him to use this time of suffering as an opportunity to do the unexpected—to allow hope, not despair, to pour out of your wounds?

Lord Jesus, may my afflictions not cause me to lose heart, but instead reveal glory.

---

11 Robinson, Jeff. "Romanian Josef Tson Recounts God's Grace Amid Suffering." Baptist Press. http://www.bpnews.net/18713 (October 24, 2017).

Day Five
GROUNDED IN LOVE

Read Ephesians 3:14–20.

1. Ephesians 3:14–17 describes our core, the most important place in each one of us. Fill in the following blanks based on verses 16 and 17.

   A. We are strengthened with power through the Holy Spirit in _____.

   B. Christ dwells in our _____ through faith.

   C. How is the heart described in CCC 2563?

2. Because life happens and hurt people hurt people, we all have wounds in our hearts. If you have ever lost someone, or experienced a painful breakup, or felt rejection, you know this to be true. We do a great job of burying our hearts under all sorts of coping mechanisms, but the hurt is still there. Deep in the heart is where we want to feel safe and secure in our identity. We want to believe in the core of our being that we belong and are accepted, but all too often this is where we are constantly trying to prove, even to ourselves, that we matter. The result? We grasp at things that can't be counted on, foolishly thinking that a good reputation, an excellent education, wealth, or being in control will keep us safe. But all of those things can be taken from us in an instant. The result? We are swimming in insecurity. Some of us hide it better than others, but it taints almost every part of our lives. In Ephesians 3:14–19, Paul prays that we would experience the antidote to this way of living. Describe it in your own words, paying special attention to verses 17–19.

3. What do the following verses tell us about these aspects of God's love for us?

The breadth of God's love: 2 Peter 3:9

The length of God's love: Philippians 2:8

The height of God's love: Romans 8:34

The depth of God's love: Ephesians 4:8–9

The word translated *comprehend* in verse 18 is a little tame compared to the original Greek. What it means is "to seize tight hold of, overtake, grasp, or wrestle." It's a picture of overpowering someone. Whom does Paul think we are wrestling with? He knows we are wrestling with ourselves. In the depths of our hearts, we are trying to prove ourselves to ourselves. So Paul challenges us to wrestle the truth into our hearts that we are loved not for anything we do but simply because we are God's beloved. It's one thing to know something as true; it's another entirely to wrestle that truth into the deepest part of you. This is a wrestling that goes on throughout our lives.

4. What will happen if we are rooted and grounded in the unconditional love of Christ, according to Ephesians 3:19? Have you ever experienced this?

Ephesians 3:19 says that the love of Christ surpasses knowledge. Combine that truth with what we learned about the heart in CCC 2563: It is beyond the grasp of our reason; only the Spirit of God can fathom and know the heart fully. This is why it takes more than reasoning for us to grasp the love of God and experience the healing of our hearts. Logic and analysis can take us only so far. There comes a point when we simply need the Holy Spirit to go to the depths of our inner self and do the healing work. Seek this level of healing. Don't settle for surface analysis or coping strategies that fail to get to the root. Would you be willing to ask God to reveal your own blind spots here?

Quiet your heart and enjoy His presence. . . . Invite the Holy Spirit into the deepest part of you.

"Now to him who can accomplish far more than all we ask or imagine, by the power at work within us, to him be glory in the church and in Christ Jesus to all generations, forever and ever." (Ephesians 3:20–21)

Holy Spirit,

Thinking about you makes me long for what's promised, and at the same time, you make me nervous. You aren't tame. I can't contain you or control you. But I can limit my experience of your power. You move and heal only when you are invited in. You empower only when you have been given permission. So I look at what is being offered to me: you, accomplishing in me far more than I could ask or imagine. You, bringing healing to places I was convinced were beyond hope. If this is true, then I want it. I am tired of just existing. I want to experience the fullness that's promised. I want to be fully alive! So you ask me to risk, to step out of my comfort zone. But you never expect me to take that leap of faith alone. Thank you for your promise in Isaiah 41:13. You grasp my right hand and say to me, "Do not fear. I will help you." You take the leap with me and you never let go.

Conclusion

"It is never too late to be what you might have been." —George Eliot

A woman who is grounded is one who has awakened to what is really important in life. She can look at the past with freedom, not regret. She can look forward with hope.

She's **grounded in reality**, recognizing that there is a battle raging between good and evil—not just in the world, but in her mind and heart.

She's **grounded in grace**, recognizing that what saves her isn't her good works, perfection, or hustle. It's grace at work in her soul.

She's **grounded in belonging**, recognizing that no matter how many times in her life she has felt abandoned or rejected, God calls her His beloved daughter.

She's **grounded in hope**, recognizing that her circumstances are only a part of the big picture, and that the deepest wounds can be healed.

She's **grounded in love**, recognizing that when she knows she is loved, she can trust God with the tender places of her heart that need His touch.

We can be grounded in these truths, and grasp hold of them when life gets upended. Or we can head off in another direction, wander in circles, and spend a lifetime wondering why nothing makes sense.

My friends, we need to experience a wakening about what will truly give us security and rootedness. It really doesn't have anything to do with where we are geographically. *Who* we are matters much more than *where* we are. It also doesn't have much to do with perfect circumstances. God has promised us that if we delight ourselves in Him, He'll give us the desires of our hearts (Psalm 37:4). The problem is, we tend to pursue that in the wrong order—we start by running after our desires, and then wind up frustrated when they don't deliver the peace we are searching for.

When we feel adrift and insecure, we need someone to anchor us and point us in the right direction. You have someone on your side who understands every conceivable challenge and heartache that may come speeding head-on in your direction. It's someone the prophet Isaiah described thousands of years ago when he wrote, "He your teacher will no longer hide Himself, but your eyes will behold your teacher. And your ears will hear a word behind you, 'This is the way, walk in it' whenever you turn to the right or the left" (Isaiah 30:20–21). This is the voice we need to listen for, and then follow with our whole hearts.

My Resolution

In what specific way will I apply what I have learned in this lesson?

Examples:

1. I want to be grounded in reality. I know that sin is real, and that it needs to be cleared out of my heart if I'm going to be able to hear God's voice. I'll go to confession this week so that any barrier that is keeping me from hearing His voice calling me beloved can be broken down by His mercy and forgiveness.

2. I want to be grounded in grace. I don't have to hustle, perform, or try to earn God's love; I already have it. When I feel myself relying on my own strength and getting worn out, I will stop and pray. I'll ask God to help me remember that it isn't all up to me. It's up to Him. I can rest. I will leave some things undone this week and trust that God can make up for where I am lacking.

3. I want to be grounded in love. I need to take a step of trust by inviting God into the places inside me that are vulnerable and hurt. I don't know how to do this

alone, so I will find someone to walk alongside me in this process—a wise friend or a professional. I will hold fast to the truth that it is not a sign of weakness to ask for help, but a sign of strength.

My resolution:

Catechism Clips

CCC 1213 Holy Baptism is the basis of the whole Christian life, the gateway to life in the Spirit *(vitae spiritualis ianua)*, and the door which gives access to the other sacraments. Through Baptism we are freed from sin and reborn as sons of God; we become members of Christ, are incorporated into the Church and made sharers in her mission: "Baptism is the sacrament of regeneration through water in the word."

CCC 1426 *Conversion* to Christ, the new birth of Baptism, the gift of the Holy Spirit and the Body and Blood of Christ received as food have made us "holy and without blemish," just as the Church herself, the Bride of Christ, is "holy and without blemish." Nevertheless the new life received in Christian initiation has not abolished the frailty and weakness of human nature, nor the inclination to sin that tradition calls *concupiscence*, which remains in the baptized such that with the help of the grace of Christ they may prove themselves in the struggle of Christian life. This is the struggle of *conversion* directed toward holiness and eternal life to which the Lord never ceases to call us.

CCC 1996 Our justification comes from the grace of God. Grace is *favor*, the free and undeserved help that God gives us to respond to his call to become children of God, adoptive sons, partakers of the divine nature and of eternal life.

CCC 1999 The grace of Christ is the gratuitous gift that God makes to us of his own life, infused by the Holy Spirit into our soul to heal it of sin and to sanctify it. It is the *sanctifying* or *deifying grace* received in Baptism. It is in us the source of the work of sanctification:

> *Therefore if any one is in Christ, he is a new creation; the old has passed away, behold, the new has come. All this is from God, who through Christ reconciled us to himself. (2 Corinthians 5:17-18)*

CCC 2563 The heart is the dwelling-place where I am, where I live; according to the Semitic or Biblical expression, the heart is the place "to which I withdraw." The heart is our hidden center, beyond the grasp of our reason and of others; only the Spirit of God can fathom the human heart and know it fully. The heart is the place of decision, deeper than our psychic drives. It is the place of truth, where we choose life or death. It is the place of encounter, because as image of God we live in relation: it is the place of covenant.

CCC 2851 "But Deliver Us From Evil" . . . In this petition [the Our Father,] evil is not an abstraction, but refers to a person, Satan, the Evil One, the angel who opposes God. The devil . . . is the one who "throws himself across" God's plan and his work of salvation accomplished in Christ.

Concupiscence: Human appetites or desires which remain disordered due to the temporal consequences of original sin, which remain even after baptism, and which produce an inclination to sin.

Jesus, I forgive

I release them to you

Lesson 5

GROUNDED TALK

Accompanying talk can be viewed by DVD or digital download purchase or access online at walkingwithpurpose.com/videos.

I. The Barrier of Unforgiveness

It's time for us to WAKE UP to the truth that we cannot _nurse_ and hold on to _grudges_ and _forgiveness_ if we want to live FEARLESS AND FREE.

What does forgiveness mean?

- It is saying that you will no longer _nurse grudges_.

- It is letting go—refusing to _rehearse_ or _____ the hurt.

- It is no longer wanting to _hurt_ because he or she hurt you.

- Forgiveness is not a one-time thing. As we learn new things about how the hurt is affecting us, we have to _keep on forgiving_

What does forgiveness NOT mean?

- Forgiveness does not mean _uncommon sense_.

- Forgiveness does not _you're off the hook_ with God.

- Forgiveness is not the same as _condoning the behavior_ what the person did to you, or allowing them unlimited access to you to do the same thing again.

II. The Barrier of Pride

The lies underlying ungodly self-reliance (pride):

I don't need ___God___. It's all up to ___me___.

III. The Power of Confession

One of the best ways for us to figure out what we need to confess is to follow the trail left by the ___emotion___ of ___hurt___.

IT'S IMPOSSIBLE TO SELF-___protect___ AND ___love___ AT THE SAME TIME.

IV. How Hurt Leads to Pride

A common sin that results from the wounds of rejection, fear, and abandonment is pride, which is self-reliance. The sin perpetuates the ___wound___, which perpetuates the ___sin___. It's a vicious cycle.

"Now to him who by the power at work within us is able to accomplish abundantly far more than all we can ask or imagine, to him be glory!" (Ephesians 3:20–21)

Discussion Questions

1. Think of a time in your life when you found (or are finding) it hard to forgive. What was (or is) the greatest obstacle? What did you learn from the talk in terms of what forgiveness is and is not?

2. What do you think of the statement "It's impossible to love and self-protect at the same time"? Do you find that you are guarded in some of your most important relationships?

3. Can you identify any lies that you agreed with during moments of pain and suffering in your life? Do you see evidence of a wound formed in your heart as a result?

THE Wrestling

THE BATTLE IN YOUR MIND & WILL

 NOTES

Lesson 6

MATURE BIBLE STUDY

Introduction

Our lessons on the Wakening have taught us who we are in Christ. Knowing we are **chosen** has helped to **ground** us in God's love. When we trust in His love, we are more likely to let Him access our hearts, and healing can begin. I pray that's been happening for you, and if it has, I know that you've probably discovered some wounds. I've found it a challenge to lean into these feelings instead of numbing or distracting myself; you probably do, too. So I'm praying that you choose instead to wake up and allow yourself to feel. Remember, you only need a little more courage than fear. Trust the process. Allow yourself to follow the trail of your hurts. Have you unearthed some things you need to address or confess? Don't wait. Dive into God's mercy. I promise, you will discover that forgiveness feels a lot like a deep breath of freedom, whether you're giving it or receiving it.

As you keep walking forward toward living Fearless and Free, you'll hear many voices and perspectives that contradict what you have just learned. I wish that wasn't the case, because it would be so much easier to live out of your true identity as a beloved daughter of God if people just affirmed and agreed with these truths. But even though the path may be rocky, you can learn to run on it with agility and grace. Psalm 18:33 promises us that God can make us as sure-footed as deer, enabling us to stand on mountain heights.

This leads us to the second part of our journey. We are going to have to renew our minds in order to grab hold of what is true and let go of what is not. Welcome to the Wrestling.

Get ready to be challenged—this is boot camp. The Wrestling requires that we enter a short, intensive, and rigorous course of training. The enemy will seek to steal what you have just gained, and the only way to protect it is to learn some self-defense techniques. We are going to identify our triggers and stop being sideswiped. Lies will be rejected and truth embraced. Fear will dissolve and trust will be our foundation.

There is no time to waste. As Pope Francis famously said, "The church cannot be herself without woman and her role. . . . The feminine genius is needed wherever we make important decisions."[12] The Church, our cities, our neighborhoods, and our families need us to be strong and mature women. The next generation is watching us, observing us, and hoping that we will fearlessly rise to the challenge.

Day One
VICTIMS NO LONGER

Read Ephesians 4:1–13.

1. A. Ephesians 4:1–3 urges us to "live in a manner worthy of the call we have received." A part of our call is to live out of our true identity as beloved daughters of God. How is that way of living described in verses 2–3?

   B. Living in that way would be easier if people treated the sensitive parts of our hearts with kid gloves. Unfortunately, certain people and circumstances set us off. What is most likely to trigger frustration and hurt in you? To get you started, here are some common emotional triggers:[13]

   feeling misunderstood
   feeling ignored
   feeling controlled
   feeling shamed
   feeling judged
   feeling rejected
   feeling treatment was unfair
   feeling alone
   feeling disrespected
   feeling unsafe
   feeling out of control
   feeling abandoned

---

[12] Spadaro, Antonio. "A Big Heart Open to God: An Interview with Pope Francis." America: The Jesuit Review. https://www.americamagazine.org/faith/2013/09/30/big-heart-open-god-interview-pope-francis (accessed October 24, 2017).

[13] A trigger is something that sets off a flashback or brings a memory to mind that takes a person back to the emotions of a traumatic event.

When we are triggered, it becomes very hard to keep our emotions from getting the better of us. Some of us fly off the handle and lash out; others withdraw; many discuss the problem with people who aren't involved in the issue at hand and are unlikely to be a part of the solution. All these responses destroy the unity Saint Paul is praying for here. This doesn't just impact the Church, although we can definitely see the damage done by division in relationships. It also hurts us personally, because lack of unity destroys community, and we need community in order to experience healing. Healing doesn't happen in isolation. It happens in the context of trustworthy, healthy relationships. We need each other.

There's little point in just identifying our triggers if all they do is give us an excuse to respond however we'd like. Author Martha Beck describes triggers as "our culture's get out of jail free card," and makes the important point that "triggers explain—they don't excuse." If we don't look at it from this perspective, we're acting like victims of our emotions. This is the response of a spiritual infant, an immature believer.

The truth? We are not victims. We can get smart about our triggers and emotions and experience redemption in places where we've habitually fallen. But we need to develop a new mind-set—an alternative way of dealing with our emotions. We're going to flesh out the "how-to" of this new mind-set in the talk following this lesson. Stay tuned.

2. Ephesians 4:7–16 addresses the way in which community can help us to grow in spiritual maturity. Answer the following questions to start teasing out the meaning of this passage.

   A. Christ measured out which gift for each of us? (v. 7)

   B. When Christ ascended on high and took prisoners captive, what did He do? (v. 8)

   C. Why did Jesus ascend and descend? (v. 10)

Jesus ascended into heaven, but not until He descended into the depths, paying the price for our sins. When He did this, He proved that there is nowhere He won't go for us. Verse 8 tells us that Jesus took prisoners captive. Unlike most conquerors, He didn't take tribute from His prisoners. Instead, He gave them gifts and filled them up. All the gifts He fills us with are meant to be shared. We are all to work together to bring one another to a place of maturity, wholeness, and healing.

3. Ephesians 4:11–12 lists some of the spiritual gifts given to specific people in the Church. How might each of these roles *done well* help the Church to mature? How might someone performing these roles help you personally as you desire to grow in maturity and wholeness?

Evangelists: share the gospel

Prophets: speak the truth

Pastors: care for the heart

Teachers: help us apply truth

Apostles: lead the charge; have bold faith that it can be done

4. Ephesians 4:13 summarizes the overall goal of this passage. Write this verse here in your own words.

A. We've been given grace and specific gifts so that the body of Christ can be built up . . .

The overall goal is for us to grow up and become mature believers. God wants to see a spirit of unity in our communities (in our homes, churches, schools, workplaces, etc.). He wants us to move "rhythmically and easily with each other, efficient and graceful . . . fully mature adults, fully developed within and without, fully alive like Christ."[14, 15]

B. In which of your relationships do you most want to see improvement in this area? Where do you see maturity, and where can you identify immaturity?

Quiet your heart and enjoy His presence. . . . He was there; He is here; He will never leave.

Dear Lord,

If I see myself as a victim of my circumstances and emotions, I will always keep myself at the center. With self in the center, unity and maturity will be unattainable. But the solution is not to ignore myself. Hurt is either transformed or transmitted. I have to deal with my pain.

Please give me the courage to let you enter the tender places in my heart to bring me healing. What I need to know is that you love me. This is a critical component of maturity. It isn't enough for me to know this in an intellectual way. I need to know it in the depth of my being. So I have to ask you, where were you when I was hurting? [Give yourself permission to pause here. Don't rush by those words. This is a significant question. Be tender with yourself as you slow down and invite God to speak to your heart.]

---

[14] The Message translation of Ephesians 4:13.
[15] Dr. Bob Schuchts, *Healing the Whole Person Workbook & Journal* (Tallahassee, FL: Dr. Bob Schuchts, 2017), 27.

My triggers can be traced back to times when I felt afraid, rejected, abandoned, ashamed, powerless, confused, or hopeless. In those dark moments, I couldn't see you. I couldn't sense your presence. So I moved into survival mode. When things happen now that trigger those same emotions, my desire to self-protect kicks in. I respond in all sorts of ways—with anger, withdrawal, perfectionism, sarcasm, drinking too much, anything that will prevent me from feeling the pain. The cycle just continues. Lord, I want to change that. I want to get off this path. My current response to my triggers blocks my maturity.

When I am triggered, help me to remember past experiences that have produced this same emotion. Help me to keep going back in my memories to see where it all began. When I prayerfully remember that time, release me from any spiritual blindness that has kept me from seeing you, present in that moment. You were *there. You have never left me. You have never forsaken me. Help me to see you there.*

What I long for is to live like your beloved daughter, because that is who I am. I belong to you. I am captivated by you, and as I gaze on your face, you fill me up with divine love. This means that when things hurt me, I can respond with humility, gentleness, and patience—not because I'm faking it, but because it's your love that flows through me. Clear the blockages, Lord. Please heal my deepest hurts, so that my relationships can be overflowing with grace and joy.

Day Two
TRUTH AND LOVE

Read Ephesians 4:14–16.

"Living the truth in love, we should grow in every way into him who is the head, Christ, from whom the whole body . . . brings about the body's growth and builds itself up in love." (Ephesians 4:15–16)

This passage reminds us that growing in maturity is a *process*. It's not something that we instantly "get" when we decide to become serious about our faith. Conversion does not equal maturity; it marks the starting point, and hopefully is the catalyst for deep transformation. This means we should expect to have to learn some basics, and put in our time. The Holy Spirit *cooperates* with us in the journey of maturity—He does not touch us with a magic wand and instantly create spiritual adults.

1. A. How are spiritual infants described in Ephesians 4:14?

Spiritual infants have trouble recognizing truth. This is not because they are unintelligent or slow. It has everything to do with how much knowledge of Scripture and Church teaching is under their belts. This is why we need to know our way around the Bible. If we don't take the time to study Scripture, we are going to be blown around by false teaching. That's a guarantee, because we are surrounded by it. In the words of Pope Emeritus Benedict XVI, "We are moving towards a dictatorship of relativism which does not recognize anything as for certain and which has as its highest goal one's own ego and one's own desires." According to our culture, there is no absolute truth, and what feels good for you is true for you. The world says that's how you should look at things. God says that's a mark of immaturity.

B. Following the thoughts of Pope Benedict, what is currently getting in the way of your own ego feeling good and your own desires being met? How are you looking at those circumstances? Are you blaming people involved? Are you growing bitter? Are you relying on yourself to see if you can somehow turn things in your favor? How might these very circumstances actually be opportunities to grow in maturity?

2. An important mark of maturity is described in Ephesians 4:15. What is it?

It might help us to understand what it means to *live the truth in love* by describing what it is not. It is *not* making up stories in our heads about what other people must be thinking and about their likely motives. But isn't this what we so often do? Something happens that triggers us. We move into self-protective mode and start to make all sorts of assumptions. It's a short distance from an assumption to a judgment. We're hurt, and instead of dealing with that hurt in truth and love, we judge the other person. In that moment, there are lies we believe about ourselves (I'm all alone; no one understands me; I'll never get out of this situation; I'm pathetic), as well as judgments we form about other people (he's so self-centered; she's hateful; he can't be trusted; she's manipulative; he's judgmental). All too often, in that moment, we close our hearts in unforgiveness.

Living the truth in love means that we take the time to unpack which lies we believe about ourselves and which judgments we are making about others. It means we start asking questions and listening so that we can better understand the other person's point of view. Social scientist Brené Brown describes this as walking into our stories of hurt. She suggests that instead of self-protecting, we put the truth *as we are perceiving it* on the table by saying, "I am feeling _____, and the story that I'm making up is _____." This takes the blame game out at the knees, and gives the other person a chance to shed light on what is true and what isn't.

This kind of communication requires vulnerability and love. It takes vulnerability to admit what you feel, and love to communicate it in a way that doesn't sound defensive or biting. Is it easy? No, but it can be a total game changer in our closest relationships. The enemy loves it when we stay up in our heads analyzing, or when we go to friends who will allow us to fill in all the blanks and describe things as we see them—which would be fine if we were always right, but all too often, we aren't.

3. A. What does Matthew 7:1–2 say about judging others?

B. Are there any judgments you are holding against someone due to a past or current experience of hurt? Are you willing to go to that person in a spirit of dialogue, seeking to understand him or her better? Sometimes it's best to enter into a conversation like this one gently, with great humility, wrapped in grace. Your softness can invite better, kinder dialogue.

Dr. Bob Schuchts has done important research into the impact of the lies and judgments that form as a result of our wounds. These lies and judgments become beliefs, which lead us to make inner vows. These vows are "promises we make to ourselves out of fear, wounds, or judgments." They are things we promise to do in order to never experience that depth of pain again. It's our game plan to save ourselves, although we rarely realize this is what we are doing. We might swear to never trust again, to never be vulnerable, to never need someone. This is what I did when I was twenty-two and I vowed I would take care of myself and not need my husband. I felt abandoned (the wound), and believed the lie that the only way I could make sure that I never felt that way again was to take care of myself and not rely on Leo. I judged him in that moment, and closed off a part of my heart. Instead of giving him grace—allowing him to be less than perfect—I made a judgment and vowed to be self-sufficient. This vow did not serve me well.

Vows like these are not rooted in truth and love; they are likely rooted in things like fear, resentment, and bitterness.

4. Can you identify any vows you have made in response to hurtful experiences?

If so, list them here.

I will always . . .

I will never . . .

We hide behind our vows. They make us feel safe. They become a protective fortress around our hearts. But something harmful happens when we make them. We enter into a survival mode that shuts out love and joy. Our lives become edited versions of what God intended them to be.

God wants us to walk in truth and love. The truth sometimes hurts. This is why we need to be rooted in His love. As we vulnerably seek to understand the bigger picture of what has gone on during our most painful memories or current circumstances, God holds us in His embrace. His love never fails us and never ends. There isn't a minute when He is not with us.

Quiet your heart and enjoy His presence. . . . He is in the heart of your story.

"We take our lead from Christ, who is the source of everything we do. He keeps us in step with each other. His very breath and blood flow through us, nourishing us so that we will grow up healthy in God, robust in love." (Ephesians 4:16, MSG)

We have this call to live with humility, gentleness, patience, and unity. We nod our heads in agreement that this is the right way to live. And then we take a moment and personalize it all, and it doesn't seem so simple. Our stories are complicated. We can't see how to unravel it all.

Isn't it beautiful that Jesus doesn't expect us to do it in our own strength? That, as Saint Julian of Norwich said, "When God sees sin, He sees pain in us"? He understands how hard it is to open our hearts, to forgive, to let go of vows and judgments. So He reminds us that He is the source of everything we do. It isn't our white-knuckling or strong resolve that allows us to live the truth in love. He does in and through us what we cannot do. That's the power of the indwelling Holy Spirit. His breath and blood flow through us. When we are dry and have nothing to offer, He says, "No worries. Just draw on the unlimited reserves of the Spirit within you. That's a more pure love than the best you can drum up anyway."

The posture we have got to get into each and every day is one of humble dependence on Him. It's a matter of opening our empty hands before Him, and asking Him to fill them with His virtues. He is behind us, before us, around us, and within us. When we say, "I can't," He agrees. Then He assures us that He can. *And He will. If only we ask.*

Day Three
A RENEWED MIND

Read Ephesians 4:17–24.

1. According to Ephesians 4:17–19, how do the Gentiles live, separated from Christ?

2. By contrast, how are we to behave? See Ephesians 4:22–24.

Unconfessed sin hardens our hearts and makes the "old self" feel like a broken-in, comfy pair of shoes. Our hardened hearts become resistant to the conviction of the Holy Spirit. It gets easier and easier to justify our behavior. This self-deception (thoughts like *I'm not so bad; Everyone is doing it; This doesn't really matter*) makes us much more susceptible to lies. One of the most common is that we are in control—that the minute we want to stop a certain behavior, we'll be able to. We don't realize that our repeated sin can fast-track us to being stuck in a stronghold. We'll explore what this looks like in the talk following this lesson.

3. Verses 20 and 21 explain the way in which we can transition from living in the futility of our minds to being renewed in the spirit of our minds. How is this process described in those verses?

If we are going to live Fearless and Free, we have got to be renewed in the spirit of our minds. This is where the battle rages fiercely. This is where worry derails us, discouragement crowds out hope, and condemnation whispers. Secret sins are played with in our minds as we relax in the false comfort that no one can see our thoughts and fantasies. The most important work in the Wrestling is done in our minds.

One of the primary ways the enemy of your soul influences you is by messing with your mind. He whispers lies, and waits to see if you will play around with the thought and agree with it. If you do, he knows he's derailed you. He also tempts you to sin, whispering things like, "It's not that big a deal; everyone does it," or "If you're just fantasizing about it, it's OK," or "You have a right to react that way. Your buttons were pushed." Then, once he gets you to sin, he loves to whisper shame.

We need to learn how to protect our minds and sort through what is the truth and what is a lie. Lies need to be rejected and truth embraced. We need to wrestle with our thoughts and discern which ones are worth keeping and which need to be tossed, instead of just letting them roam around. Why would we allow a thought to stay in our heads that contradicts the thoughts that are in God's?

4. The battle in the mind is described in 2 Corinthians 10:3–5. Read the passage and answer the following questions.

    A. Describe our weapons for the battle:

    B. What are we destroying?

    C. What do we do with every thought?

We aren't born knowing how to wield the weapons God has provided for us. Mindfulness, a good self-esteem, and pure grit will help to a certain extent, but they will never be powerful enough to win the battle of the mind. Learning how to take every thought captive in obedience to Christ will be the focus of the talk following this lesson, and it is one of the most critical teachings of this Bible study. Please do not skip it.

Quiet your heart and enjoy His presence. . . . Let Him baptize your thoughts and imagination.

"Do not conform yourselves to this age but be transformed by the renewal of your mind that you may discern what is the will of God, what is good and pleasing and perfect." (Romans 12:2)

As we learn to recognize the whispers of the enemy and reject them, we will be strengthened and grow in maturity. Dwelling on truth will change our outlook on life and the decisions we make. We are promised in John 8:32 that when we know the truth, it will set us free.

Once we are dwelling on what is true, we need that truth to enter our hearts. We become fully alive to the extent that truth has taken root deep within. Lies keep us dead in despair. Truth reminds us that a fresh start is always possible and that we have spiritual strength that can carry us through.

Dear Lord,

I recognize that I'm in the midst of a battle. But you have not left me to fight alone. You are with me—behind me, before me, all around me, and most important, within me. I can be fearless—not because of my innate strength, but because you dwell within me through the Holy Spirit. You can walk me through anything. Help me to remember that shrinking back, stepping off the path that you have set me on, will not result in blessing. My compromise won't bring safety or protection; it simply means I am walking away from your will. I want to stay under the umbrella of your protection. Help me to stay faithful. I need your grace.

Day Four
THE NEW SELF

1. A. How are we told to behave in Ephesians 4:25-29, and why are we told we should act this way?

B. How is true love described in 1 Corinthians 13:6?

As we saw in Day Two, we need to learn how to speak the truth in love (Ephesians 4:15). A big part of putting off the old self (Ephesians 4:22) and putting on the new self (Ephesians 4:24) is being transformed in this way. We don't just tell the truth, we *rejoice* with the truth, because we know that the more truthful we are, the more we become women of true integrity, and in doing so, we become our truest selves.

But we don't do this in isolation. The kind of transformation that the book of Ephesians is describing takes place in the context of community. It shouldn't surprise us that the deep healing and restoration we need requires closeness to others. We have ended up where we are not just because of our individual choices, but because of the ways we've been shaped by our first community, our families. The way we were treated there has impacted and shaped us. We need an equally close community to help us mature spiritually. This means being close enough to people of faith that they can speak truth into our lives about areas where we need to grow and change. What others hopefully will do for us, we will ideally do for others.

Why do we shy away from telling the truth? If we're honest, we often don't tell the truth because we don't want to experience the unpleasantness of delivering unwelcome words. We may say we're being loving when we hold back truth, but we are really just looking out for ourselves. Theologian Tim Keller brings an interesting perspective on this in his study of Ephesians. He makes the point that love without truth telling isn't about love. It's about you. When we don't speak the truth, we disempower others because we are denying them reality. It's critical that we look at what we are trying to do with our words. We can be very careful to technically tell the truth, but we design our words with the intent to deceive—to put people off the scent.[16] This was exactly what I was doing when I crafted responses to "How are you?" in such a way that no one would dig deeper into what was really going on. I was an expert at putting people off the scent, and as a result, I denied the very people I loved most the reality they needed to hear. I thought I was being loving both to myself and to them, but I was actually disempowering us and preventing us from growing healthier relationships.

---

[16] Tim Keller, "What We Are Becoming: Transforming Love: Love and Truth" (lecture, Redeemer Presbyterian Church, New York, June 19, 2016).

C. Can you see any examples or tendencies in your own life to say something factually true that is designed to deceive? Do you struggle with half-truths, falling into the trap of saying "you always" or "you never" when you communicate?

If we refuse to speak truth to one another, instead saying that things don't matter or talking behind people's backs, we won't see where we need to grow. Our ability to self-deceive is rather off the charts, unfortunately. But if we only get truth without love, we'll just block out what's being said. We need both, in equal doses.

2. A. What instructions does Saint Paul give about anger in Ephesians 4:26–27?

B. Is anger always a sin? See Ephesians 4:26 and John 2:13–17.

There is righteous anger and unrighteous anger. When something wells up within us that says, "This is not right," there is always a chance that we are judging correctly and we have seen something wrong or unjust. But righteous anger doesn't focus on *our* rights; it focuses on the rights of *others*. Jesus is the supreme example of this: When He was angry in the temple, it was zeal for *His Father's* house that consumed Him (John 2:17). It is not a sin to be angry about injustice. It can become a sin, however, when we decide that we should be the ones to judge. Both the judgment and the handing out of consequences are things we are to leave to God.

Unrighteous anger is one of the seven deadly sins and is rooted in a deep desire for power and control. When we feel powerless and out of control, anger surges and tempts us. In a talk at the Healing the Whole Person conference, Dr. Bob Schuchts said, "We want to satiate our pain right now instead of waiting for who God is. For Him to show up." We blow up and we lash out, which might make us feel better temporarily. But behind our actions is a lack of trust in God. We don't trust that He will set things right—at least not on our timetable—so we rely on ourselves to feel better about things. What do we find at the root of this? Ungodly self-reliance.

So where else can we go with the emotion of anger? We head back to Ephesians 4:15 and 25. We speak the truth in love. We take necessary action, but we trust God to be the judge and jury.

C. Is there a relationship in your life in which you are struggling with anger? Do you believe your anger is righteous or unrighteous? Is there an action you could take to help bring restoration to the situation at hand and to the relationship? Are you willing to do what it takes to help you both grow in maturity? Are you open to receiving honest feedback that might feel critical or hurtful but that could also be helpful?

I've just got to hit pause here, because actually living this out is so hard. It's actually *too* hard—impossible to do in our own strength. But this is where God enters the picture, tenderly and yet with tremendous strength. Picture Him cupping your face in His hands. Listen to Him say, "I know. I understand," because He truly does. He sees the injustice and weeps with you. Far from demanding that you discount it or act like it doesn't matter, He asks if you will let Him fight for you. If you let Him, I promise you, He will show up. It may be in hidden, mysterious ways. But He will never fail to come and fight for His beloved daughter—you.

3. Ephesians 4:29 takes all these instructions and goes deeper in terms of how we are to live them out. We know we're to speak the truth, but what else should our words be accomplishing according to this verse?

This verse is pointing to the motive behind our words. It isn't enough to just tell the truth, and it isn't enough to just deliver the news in a kind tone of voice. Building up the other person needs to be our motive. *Why* are we telling the truth? Is it to make the point? To wash our hands of a situation? To show we are right and superior? To punish with our words? If so, we should stop talking. Now is not the time to deliver the truth. Why? Because our hearts aren't in the right place.

Unless we have a vision for where we want the other person to be as a result of our words, unless our deepest desire is for him or her to be built up, unless we want to draw closer in relationship—then our motives are not pure. Our words might not be foul or unkind, but they fall short of the kind of communication that brings about transformation. It doesn't mean the truth shouldn't eventually be told, just not by you at this time.

Quiet your heart and enjoy His presence.... You are offered a fresh start as a new creation in Christ.

Speaking the truth in love frees us to live like the new self we truly are. Russell Willingham describes this process of transformation:

> *If you move in the direction of truth and honesty, this is what your life will look like: you will not need to hide, you will seek out other honest people whom you can trust with your brokenness, you will know that brokenness is a permanent part of the human condition . . . you will be gracious toward other broken people instead of critical and self-righteous . . . you will live in constant gratitude for a God who accepts you, brokenness and all . . .[17]*

Every day, we should begin with an awareness of our own brokenness and our need for others to speak truth to us. Only then will we be able to be humble, Christlike truth tellers.

When we are baptized as God's beloved daughters, we are anointed as prophets (and priests and kings). As a prophet, Jesus spoke and embodied divine truth. As the body of Christ, we are called to do the same. Envisioning and communicating where a loved one could be if he or she gave God full control of his or her life to God is a form of prophesying. "Those who prophesy speak to other people for their upbuilding and encouragement and consolation" (1 Corinthians 14:3).

This is one way we live as a resurrected, Easter people. We are people of hope who cast vision for those who can't see past brokenness.

God wants us to be aware of our brokenness and need for Him, but in the words of my friend Heather Khym, He doesn't want us carrying our cross around in circles. We should be moving forward, toward the healing. That process can feel a lot like a crucifixion. But we do it all with our eyes on the resurrection. We grab hold of the promise that God is always in the process of creating something new and restoring what is broken. The end of the story is not the pain. It's new life!

---

[17] Russell Willingham, *Breaking Free* (Downers Grove, IL: InterVarsity Press, 1999), 126–37.

Dear Lord,

It's hard for me to look past my problems and the things that I see are wrong in people I love. Recognizing our mess and our need for you isn't so tough. But catching a vision of who we could be? That's a little harder. That requires hope.

Thank you for giving me hope—for being the embodiment of hope. I don't have to conjure it up. I just have to lean into you, and ask you for the vision of what you are calling us all to be. Grant me the vision to see who I can become. Help me to have that same ability to see beyond current circumstances when I pray for and speak to those I love.

May I pick up my cross and surge forward in the power of the Holy Spirit. May I not settle for mediocrity, stopping halfway up the hill. Give me the strength and hope to faithfully continue on the journey. "It is not that I have already taken hold of it or have already attained perfect maturity, but [help me to] continue my pursuit in hope that I may possess it . . . forgetting what lies behind but straining forward to what lies ahead, [may I] continue my pursuit toward the goal, the prize of God's upward calling, in Christ Jesus" (Philippians 3:12–14).

Day Five
GET MOVING UP THE HILL

Read Ephesians 4:30–32.

1. A. What are we asked not to do in Ephesians 4:30?

   B. What is one of the roles of the Holy Spirit, according to John 16:7–8? (The Holy Spirit is referred to as the Advocate in this passage.)

The Holy Spirit shines a light into our hearts and reveals our sin. As we experience His conviction, we have a choice how we will respond. The light of the Holy Spirit often hurts our eyes; too often, we look away. We distract ourselves. We justify our behavior. We move on. When we react like this, the Holy Spirit is grieved.

The opposite of grieving the Holy Spirit is obedience. As we focus on the importance of growing in spiritual maturity, there is no way around this step. We can become open and aware of our brokenness. We can be truth tellers and truth receivers. *But what are we doing with that truth?* Are we just becoming smarter sinners?

Make no mistake, the Wrestling requires a battle with the will. Self-awareness is not the goal. We are called to mature, to grow up. And that means we get serious about rooting out sin in our lives. We stop blaming others and making excuses. We start taking God at His word. When the Holy Spirit says something needs to be confessed, gotten rid of, or conquered, we acquiesce and we do it *right away*. We don't play around with sin in our minds or in our hearts. We *root it out*. It's a painful process (pruning always is), and it's not always linear. It requires perseverance.

Far too many of us are sitting down halfway up the hill to maturity. We've decided we like the view. Our level of holiness seems good enough—it's not like we want everyone thinking we're weird. There are plenty of people lower down with bigger areas of sin, so we figure we're OK. We've got some good company around us— friends who make us feel comfortable and assure us that as long as we're generally *inclined* toward God, He'll be merciful to us. Not to mention, there's always tomorrow. No need to be all intense about holiness today.

And the Holy Spirit weeps over us.

2. A. If we are serious about not grieving the Holy Spirit, if we truly want to become mature daughters of God, what will we root out of our hearts and lives? See Ephesians 4:31.

B. What will we make sure is found in our hearts and lives? See Ephesians 4:32.

Do you know how I usually respond when I read lists of sins and virtues? My eyes kind of glaze over. It's not that I don't agree with what the Bible is saying. It's just that the sin I am playing around with at that moment is often not found in the list. And I just keep on behaving as I was before. Maybe my mind wanders over to someone I know who definitely should be reading and applying those verses, and then I spend a little chunk of time dwelling on her sins. That's pretty messed up, but I'm just being honest.

So if I am really serious about growing up as a Christian, I am not going to just answer the questions in the Bible study. I'm going to take some additional steps. When I have done the following four things, my eyes have been opened. I've been humbled, I've been led to confession, and I get back on the journey up the hill.

Here's my list:

1. I beg the Holy Spirit to convict me of my secret sins. I ask Him to speak to me clearly about the things that I hide and ignore.

2. I go to confession. The cobwebs of sin make it hard for me to hear His voice.

3. I ask people closest to me what it's like to be on the other side of me—what it's like to experience me. I am always surprised by their answers. It turns out that what I thought I hid well is actually leaking out. I am, as a result, less delightful than I imagined I was. My own perspective is skewed. Who knew? Not me, until I asked them. A note about this one: It's hard for people to speak truth into our lives if we're defensive. People who love us will probably be afraid of what their honesty might cost them. Because of this, we often have to ask for this feedback several times, and show in between those times that we genuinely want to grow and be transformed.

4. I ask someone I trust to hold me accountable in my area of sin and weakness (specifically, or as specifically as possible).

C. Who is close enough to you to be able to give honest feedback about areas where you need to grow? Are you willing to ask him or her? As you ponder these questions, remember how treasured and valued you are by God. There is nothing you can do to increase or decrease that love. His love for you is not at stake in this exercise, but your freedom is. Sin keeps you in bondage; confession and forgiveness break the chains. Obedience allows you to fly.

3. What do the following verses teach you about sin?

Genesis 4:7

Romans 6:12

Romans 6:16

Getting serious about obeying God is one of the best self-defense techniques imaginable. When we play fast and loose with what God has told us to do, we crack open the door and invite the enemy in to play. We become enslaved to things that we thought we could control, and misery results. Brick by brick, sin builds up a wall in our hearts. It gets harder to connect with God. The wall of sin causes lies to be so much easier to hear. The Father's gentle voice becomes a faint whisper that we can't quite make out.

Surrendering our will to God and obeying seems like the hardest thing imaginable at times, but what we can't lose sight of is the fact that everyone surrenders to something. Whatever it is that you most desire, whatever you are willing to sacrifice for, you are surrendered to that. Only God loves you unconditionally. Only God is guaranteed to never leave you or forsake you. Only God knows everything about your past and all that is to come in your future. So who better to write the story of your life? Who is more worthy of trust than the One who made you and has brought you this far?

4. What should motivate us to freely forgive others? See Ephesians 4:32.

Another perspective that helps us to forgive is to look at our wounds differently. Most people see trauma and pain as something devoid of any good. When we are able to see redemption and healing in spite of and sometimes because of our pain, something shifts. We are better able to recognize another's brokenness, and this causes us to feel compassion. This is one way to check if we've truly forgiven someone—are we able to look at this person in his or her brokenness? At the same time, we need to be honest about the pain inflicted. We do not say the pain or trauma didn't matter. We say, "Yes, you did hurt me." We name what was taken from us, the debt we feel we are owed. But instead of shaking the person, saying, "Pay me what you owe me," we recognize the enormous debt we owe to God. We recognize that we all are debtors, and that we all need mercy. This is what allows us to make an act of the will and choose to forgive. When we do this, another shackle is loosened and we begin to taste freedom.

Quiet your heart and enjoy His presence. . . . He calls you onward and upward.

"The world offers you comfort. But you were not made for comfort. You were made for greatness."
—Pope Benedict XVI

Wrestling sin out of our lives will never come easily. It will always be more comfortable to ignore it, sweep it under the rug, or put off doing anything about it. But we were made for more.

If we are going to experience the more we were made for, we will have to embrace two truths that on the surface might seem contradictory.

On the one hand, we are to abide in Christ and let Him do His transforming work within us. This is described beautifully in 1 Thessalonians 5:23–24: "May the God of peace Himself sanctify you entirely; and may your spirit and soul and body be kept sound and blameless at the coming of our Lord Jesus Christ. The one who calls you is faithful, and he will do this."

But that's not all. As we embrace the "both . . . and" of the Bible, we turn to Colossians 3:8–10 and read, "But now you must get rid of all such things—anger, wrath, malice, slander, and abusive language from your mouth. Do not lie to one another, seeing that you have stripped off the old self with its practices and have clothed yourselves with the new self."

Both *are true. The Holy Spirit makes us holy from within.* And *we cooperate in the process by making the choice to obey God.*

If we want to experience the greatness we were created for, we will hold these two truths in holy tension. We will fully surrender to the Holy Spirit's work within us, which requires only that we be still. At the same time, we will tirelessly guard our hearts, minds, and bodies against anything that would "make room for the devil" (Ephesians 4:27). In doing so, we will fearlessly keep climbing.

Dear Lord,

The comfort of mediocrity makes the hill to holiness look impossible to climb. But I desire greatness. I don't want to miss out on the real life that I was created for. So I echo Saint Teresa of Ávila's prayer: "Knowing that the strength given by obedience usually lessens the difficulty of things that seem impossible, I resolve to carry out the task very willingly, even though my human nature seems greatly distressed. . . . May [God] in whose mercy I trust and who has helped me in other, more difficult things so as to favor me, do this work for me . . ."[18]

"Strengthen the weak hands, and make firm the feeble knees. Say to those who are of a fearful heart, Be strong, do not fear! Here is your God . . . He will come and save you." (Isaiah 35:3)

And so, strengthened by you, may I rise up and scale the heights. Amen.

---

[18] St. Teresa of Ávila, *The Interior Castle* (New York/Mahwah, NJ: Paulist Press, 1979).

Conclusion

"If you are what you should be, you will set the whole world ablaze!" —*Saint Catherine of Siena*

What a difference we can make in our world if we are willing to do whatever it takes to become mature daughters of God. For too long we have settled for being less than who we were created to be. We've accepted our lot in life and given up on experiencing the resurrection this side of heaven. We've sat down on the hill, enduring our crosses as badges of honor, when God has been asking us to climb the hill to Calvary to experience healing. We aren't supposed to stay stuck in Good Friday. As Saint John Paul II said, "We are Easter people and alleluia is our song!"[19] Experiencing resurrection and newness of life is our birthright as children of God.

So why do we stay in the dead places? For one thing, getting up and moving out of mediocrity and numbness can feel strange. We are exercising muscles that have been at rest. Taking a look at our triggers and going deeper to see where they come from feels foreign and unsettling. Shedding the old self and asking God to unearth our hidden sins is scary.

Leaving behind immaturity can mean letting some relationships go, and that is painful. We have some good company midway up the hill. The friends who encourage us to settle for "good enough" provide comfort and soothe us. The people up ahead might not seem like much fun and can appear intimidating. The temptation to go back or stay lukewarm makes the dead places seem deceptively safe.

Determining to do whatever it takes to grow up requires courage and grit. Thankfully, God has not left us to go it alone. The grace that we need is always on offer. It is there for the asking. We are promised in 1 Timothy 1:7, "God has not given us a spirit of timidity but a spirit of power and love and self-control." He's given us His Spirit, and He's given us each other. So let's link arms, knowing we are stronger in community, and commit to climbing the hill to maturity together.

"Since we are surrounded by so great a cloud of witnesses, let us also lay aside every weight and the sin that clings so closely, and let us run with perseverance the race that is set before us, looking to Jesus, the pioneer and perfecter of our faith." (Hebrews 12:1–2)

---

[19] Saint John Paul II, Angelus (Adelaide, Australia, November 30, 1986), The Holy See, https://w2.vatican.va/content/john-paul-ii/en/angelus/1986/documents/hf_jp-ii_ang_19861130.html

My Resolution

In what specific way will I apply what I have learned in this lesson?

Examples:

1. I feel I am stuck in the pain of my past. Because I desire to be free, I will find a Christian therapist who will help me begin the process of healing. I will trust God's timeline on this journey, and commit to cooperating with the work of the Holy Spirit in my heart.

2. I need to communicate honestly about a difficult situation with a loved one. I resolve to go to adoration to prayerfully look at my motives, and ask God to help me speak the truth in love.

3. God has convicted me of a sin that I would like to hide. But I know that hiding and darkness is an environment that encourages the growth of sin, not the death of it. I will find a trusted friend to hold me accountable in this area of my life and go to confession to receive forgiveness and strength to resist sinning again.

My resolution:

NOTES

Lesson 7

MATURE TALK

Accompanying talk can be viewed by DVD or digital download purchase or access online at walkingwithpurpose.com/videos.

I. WHAT IS THE PROBLEM?

The parable of the seed and the sower in Matthew 13:1-43.

We have got to learn how to be _____ and _____ in our minds.

II. WRESTLING WITH STRONGHOLDS

"For, although we are in the flesh, we do not battle according to the flesh, for the *weapons of our battle are not of flesh but are enormously powerful, capable of destroying fortresses. We destroy arguments, and every pretension raising itself against the knowledge of God, and take every thought captive in obedience to Christ." 2 Corinthians 10:3–5 (NAB)

Hurt -> Inner Vows -> Strongholds

We must discipline ourselves and develop a different mind-set. We need to stop and ask ourselves:

Based on our knowledge of God, what do we know to be true of Him?

Hebrews 4:12

Proverbs 4:20–23

III. WRESTLING FOR REAL

A. Wrestling in Prayer

B. Wrestling with the "I Declares"

"The extent to which truth enters our hearts is the extent to which we come fully alive." Dr. Bob Schuchts[20]

Discussion Questions

1. In the talk, strongholds are defined as "places we go to find our security and safety when we feel threatened. We go to those places instead of going to God. In that moment, we choose to rely on ourselves rather than on Him." Can you identify any strongholds in your own life? Have you experienced a stronghold no longer being something you control, but rather something that is mastering you? Keep in mind that many strongholds are deceptively beautiful and often affirmed by others.

2. Can you identify any arguments or lies that are seeking to draw you away from what you know to be true about God? What lie about God's character tempts you to seek security in things other than Him?

3. Which of the I Declares resonated most with you? Which did you find hardest to believe? You will find them in Appendix 5.

---

[20] Bob Schuchts, "Prayer for Inner Healing." Lecture, Healing the Whole Person Conference, Tallahassee, FL, March 14, 2017.

Lesson 8

PASSIONATE BIBLE STUDY

Introduction

We were never meant to go it alone—God has wired us for connection. Our desire to be known and to belong has divine origins. A yearning for intimacy was placed in our hearts by our Creator. God knows that He is the only One who will perfectly fulfill that longing, so He pursues us with fervent faithfulness. The lover of our soul is passionate about nothing getting in the way of that closeness.

Because of His single-minded focus on what will help us to flourish, God is very clear in Scripture about what will keep us from experiencing the greatest closeness to Him. He is on our side, not only pointing out what we need to avoid, but giving us the strength to do what He asks. But we need to cooperate with His grace at work in our souls. God gives us all that we need, but we must make the decision to enter the battle and wrestle with anything that threatens our inheritance as beloved daughters.

In Ephesians 5:1–6, we'll see that we need to wrestle with our desires. What is ultimately best for us is often not what we feel like doing. Our desires tend to lean toward the comfortable, the easy, and the short-term gain. We have to battle our own will every day with passion and vigor if we're going to experience the abundance that God has for us.

We also wrestle with the darkness, which we'll look at in Ephesians 5:7–20. The enemy loves for us to live in the shadows, but we are challenged to battle through the confusion of the gray and murky and live in the light.

Fierce battles rage in the realm of relationships. It seems that things intensify when it comes to issues within families. Unquestionably, much of our wrestling will occur as we navigate hurt, betrayal, disappointment, and anger with those closest to us. Ephesians 5:21–6:4 will give us principles to help us navigate these relationships.

But these insights will have little effect on us unless we are passionate about winning the daily battle within our minds and hearts. It requires waking up with determination and pressing on toward victory.

What are you most passionate about?

If you're truly passionate about something, you're willing to sacrifice other valuables for its sake.

My prayer for each one of us is that *we would decide that we are passionate about growing in holiness and closeness to God*. My hope is that even though doubts linger, we would trust that He is the only One who will never leave us, and that He is *good*. He is worth any sacrifice because He is the only One who will truly satisfy our longing hearts.

I believe we are tired of living half-heartedly when the wholehearted life beckons. For too long, we've felt trapped by patterns of behavior that we know are destructive. I believe we are ready to be free. Fear of losing people's approval has caused us to compromise. It's time for us to sacrifice their applause, no matter how good it feels in the moment, in order to make the choices that lead to peace and joy. I believe we are ready to live for an audience of One.

May our passion for holiness propel us into the battle with a laser-sharp focus on what is at stake. No longer settling for just surviving, may we wrestle to the ground and kick to the curb anything that stands in the way of our closeness to Christ and maturity.

Day One
DESIRE

"Living the Christian life is not a matter of repressing our desires, but of redeeming them." — *Christopher West*

Read Ephesians 5:1–5.

1. A. As beloved daughters of God, what are we called to do in Ephesians 5:1–2?

   B. How was Jesus' sacrificial offering to God described in Ephesians 5:2?

The sacrifice that Jesus offered to God was a life of perfect obedience to Him and radical love for people. That intoxicating combination released a fragrance that was irresistible to people who were searching for belonging and meaning. When we imitate Christ's forgiveness and love, our lives have the same effect.

2. A. If we are imitating God, which things will not be found in our lives? See Ephesians 5:3–4.

B. How did Saint Paul intensify his explanation of what it takes to be like Christ in Ephesians 5:3?

In the words of Peter Williamson in his commentary on Ephesians, "[Suggestive talk] coarsens us and gives immorality a false attractiveness. It desensitizes us to God's commandments, weakening inhibitions against wrongdoing, and conceals the ruin in families and heartbreak in relationships that accompany adultery and other forms of sexual immorality."[21] Even when we think we're just passively being entertained, something is going on deep within us. We laugh at things we wouldn't dream of doing in real life, and without realizing it, we become desensitized to sin. Later, it makes it a lot easier to justify little compromises because we've allowed our consciences to be dulled. Something has been introduced to our minds and brings us nearer to actually doing it.

When our consciences are dulled, we are less apt to feel guilty. As a result, we keep sinning, and are unlikely to confess it. Each sin is like a brick, building a wall between us and the voice of the Holy Spirit. He's there, trying to guide us toward the choices that will bring us happiness, but His voice is faint. The result? We wander down roads leading to nowhere. Our choices about what we watch, listen to, and talk about truly matter.

C. Are there any shows or forms of entertainment that you need to stop watching? Do you need to curb some sexual humor? Are there any relationships in which you are especially prone to speak carelessly?

---

[21] Williamson, *Ephesians*, 139.

3. A. If even talking about immorality or impurity is a concern, we can be sure that what we actually do with our bodies matters. We're surrounded by voices that insist our sexuality should be explored outside the confines of marriage. Most people would say that following God's instructions about sex is an archaic response to our bodies' natural inclinations. Yet wise voices, some quite young, rise up with a different perspective. The following excerpt from a letter from someone I know was written by a loving sister out of concern for her sibling:

> Sharing a bed with someone without covenanting before God to love that person in sickness and in health, for better or for worse, for richer or for poorer, until death separates you, is a sham. . . .
>
> I firmly believe that the very essence of marriage is a binding commitment. The very essence of living together is *no* binding commitment. That's why living together can't be a trial for marriage, because in everything that matters the two conditions are opposites. And that's why not having a binding commitment is less like training for marriage and more like training for divorce.
>
> And as for sexual compatibility, no one can properly learn to have sex outside a marriage: there isn't any time, you have no security in the relationship, and mistakes are humiliating because—in essence—you're on an audition.

God understands our desire for intimacy and belonging; He's the One who placed those desires deep in our hearts to begin with! He knows we are prone to look for them in the wrong places, so He gives us "guardrails"—moral guidelines that if followed can keep us from being deeply wounded. When He limits the exploration of our sexuality to marriage, He is not trying to ruin our fun. It's His protection as a good, good Father. He knows the inevitable hurt that lies on the other side of the sexual sin that appears "fun," and He longs to shield you from it.

God wants our security to be grounded in our identity as beloved daughters. He longs for us to grow in maturity so that we become more like Jesus. As we mature, His plan is for us to grow in purity.[22] As we read in Ephesians 5:4, "Immorality or any impurity or greed must not even be mentioned among you." If we are aware of our impurity, reading this can cause us to feel covered with shame. If we aren't aware, is it possible we are lying to ourselves about the true condition of our hearts here? But what can we do about it? How can we come to be pure?

We don't grow in purity by redefining sin and saying that it's all OK.

---

[22] Schuchts, *Be Healed*, 90.

We don't grow in purity by standing under a weight of condemnation and shame.

We become pure as we rest in God's embrace. This is what happens in the sacrament of reconciliation. We confess, God opens His arms and welcomes us, and He forgives us. That forgiveness heals us and makes us pure.

Is there an area of your sexual life where you desire healing and forgiveness? Be assured, God's stance toward you is one of compassion. His heart aches over any pain you may have experienced in this tender area. If there is sin you need to confess, remember that there is no sin that is out of the reach of His forgiving, redeeming hand; He already knows it. He just longs for you to climb into His lap and share your heart with Him.

B. Has someone hurt you or stolen from your innocence or purity? I promise, God will restore everything that the enemy used to harm you. Have you acted in ways that devalued your body or that have brought regret and shame into your heart in the area of sexuality?

If these questions are striking a chord in your heart, I invite you to pause and acknowledge the gravity of this. I encourage you to seek out counseling or a trusted person for presence. Sometimes we just need someone to walk with us to approach the throne of grace.

Dear Lord, I desire healing in this area of my life:

With Jesus, there is always a fresh start, a new beginning. Whether we are in our current situation because of our own choices or because others have abused us, Jesus restores our dignity, completely.

Quiet your heart and enjoy His presence. . . . His love will redeem your desires.

"Open your minds and hearts to the beauty of all that God has made and to His special, personal love for each one of you." —Saint John Paul II

It all really boils down to trust. That was the problem way back in the Garden of Eden. The serpent spoke doubt into Eve's heart, suggesting that God really was holding out on her. Underneath the serpent's words was the question, "Is God really good?" Eve wasn't sure, agreed with the lie, and took matters into her own hands. She wrestled, but in her own strength; it wasn't enough. It would have been a game changer if she had reached out to God in prayer, but she relied on herself instead. Women and men have been doing the same thing ever since that fateful day.

What is needed if we are going to be imitators of God? It begins with a willingness to trust. Unless we believe that God is for us, that He wants what is best for us, and that He is powerful enough to make it happen, we'll keep doing things our own way. We'll ignore his guidance and careen through life, being wounded over and over again.

Trust is built as we take the time to look at the character of God and then personalize the implications of who He is. Prayerfully read these attributes of God, asking Him to help you believe that this is who He is for you, personally.

God is faithful.
Lord, people have left me. I've experienced betrayal and rejection. Help me to separate you from my experiences with those who have hurt me. May I not judge your character by my circumstances or the reactions and choices of others, but judge the circumstances in light of your character.

God is good.
Lord, I sometimes struggle to believe that your way is the best way. I wonder if you are holding out on me. Help me to remember that all good gifts come from you. Every ounce of joy, pleasure, and fulfillment that I have experienced has come from your hand. Help me to believe that you desire, more than anything, to bless me. But as a good Father, you will not give me things that you, in all your wisdom, know would ultimately hurt me. Help me to be patient and wait for the best gifts instead of settling for what is right in front of me in the moment.

God is here, right now.

Lord, help me to believe that you are here. You are not repulsed by me; you love me. When I come to you with my sin, you do not withdraw from me. You press in, cleansing and healing my wounds. Not only are you here right now, you have always *been with me. There is not a memory I can visit where you were not present. I may not have seen you, but you were there.*

God is all-powerful.

Lord, with your unlimited power, there is nothing you cannot redeem. We never need to finish as we've started, because you can intersect seemingly hopeless situations and do the miraculous. You are far more creative than I am, and your solutions go way beyond the best things I can come up with. I trust that if you can create breathtaking sunsets, majestic mountains, and shimmering oceans, you are a better artist than I am. I give you the paintbrush, and ask you to create a masterpiece out of my life. Shape my desires so that I want what you want, when you want it, how you want it.

Day Two
LIGHT

Read Ephesians 5:6–14.

1. A. In Ephesians 5:6, we are warned not to be deceived by what?

As we learned in Lesson 6: Mature, not only should we avoid being deceived by empty arguments, we are to "destroy arguments and every pretension raising itself against the knowledge of God, and take every thought captive to Christ" (2 Corinthians 10:4–5).

What sort of empty arguments is Saint Paul talking about? We can recognize an empty argument when we see that it is pitting itself against what we know to be true about God. These arguments often make some degree of sense, but are a twisting of the truth. They are a thin coating of reason that covers up a lie.

The enemy loves to play around with words in this way. It started in the Garden of Eden when he twisted God's words with Adam and Eve. This is still his game. Just look at the way our words have been manipulated to make sin seem less serious: Words like *lifestyle*, *sexual orientation*, *reproductive rights*, and *affairs* are far less convicting than *greed*, *sodomy*, *abortion*, and *adultery*.

The enemy was called a "false lover" by Saint Ignatius, because even as he entices us to look at things from his perspective instead of God's, even as he lures us with temptation, he wants to keep it a secret. In the words of Father Timothy Gallagher, "the enemy seeks to shroud his deceits... [but] our way of responding... will determine much of the subsequent course of the temptation, deception, or attack: whether these will diminish or increase their hold on us."[23] We are not victims of the enemy's deceits. We have a choice to either agree with his perspective or call him out on his lies. When we respond by asking ourselves, "Is this real or not real? Is this the truth or a lie?" we will significantly diminish the enemy's ability to mess with us.

Taking every thought captive to Christ (2 Corinthians 10:5) means that we hear an argument (or lie) and immediately ask ourselves, "Is this true?" We challenge the argument or lie and compare it to what we read in Scripture and Church teachings. If we're not going to be deceived by empty arguments, then we are going to have to call things what God calls them. When we do this, it is a kick in the teeth to the enemy. In Saint Ignatius' rules for discernment, he reminds us that the enemy is essentially weak. Father Gallagher explains further:

> When confronted firmly and decisively, the enemy is weak and helpless. If dedicated persons refuse "to be afraid and lose heart" and choose to do "what is diametrically opposed" to the enemy's temptations, then "it is proper to the enemy to weaken and lose heart, fleeing and ceasing his temptations." ... **The enemy is ... essentially a coward** [emphasis added]. Like a coward, he will only attack when met with weakness; when resisted firmly, he flees.[24]

Truth always liberates us. This is why we make the effort to *find out what God calls sin* and then do all we can to live the way He says is best. We are surrounded by people celebrating the very things God tells us to run from. He challenges us to choose Him even when the voices are loud and convincing.

To make matters trickier, we live in a world of sound bites. We consume information quickly and in bullet points. We skim the surface instead of digging for underlying facts and deeper understanding. As a result, when we encounter a Church teaching or a commandment in the Bible, we think to ourselves, "*What?* You have got to be kidding me. No one thinks that is a big deal. This is archaic. This is out of touch." Most people stop right there, because they figure they have enough info (gleaned from scratching the surface) to make a "good enough" choice.

---

[23] Timothy M. Gallagher, OMV, *The Discernment of Spirits: An Ignatian Guide for Everyday Life* (New York: Crossroad Publishing Company, 2005), 150.
[24] Ibid., 153.

But you, my friend, are doing the opposite of this. You are digging deep. You are committed to the freedom found only on the other side of the lie. You are exploring new ways of looking at life. Thank you for persevering in this study. Thank you for wrestling with concepts and ideas that may be foreign or confusing to you. Thank you for pressing on even when doubts play in your mind. Don't let the doubts and questions discourage you. They may simply be evidence that you are forging new spiritual ground. This is a part of the Wrestling.

Your steadfast engagement in these lessons reveals your desire for something better, something more. It can also indicate a real growth in humility. Instead of claiming to have it all figured out, you are acknowledging that God has a higher perspective, and that taking some time to listen to Him leads you closer to understanding that perspective. Too few of us are willing to climb this mountain, but those who do are promised a fuller view and a fuller life.

B. Can you identify any arguments that are taking up space in your head and heart? Will you commit to digging deeper and learning more about what God has to say about this issue?

C. Father Timothy Gallagher wrote that the enemy is essentially a coward. When we resist him, he flees. What essential truth about the enemy is found in 1 John 4:4? (Note: in this passage, the enemy is referred to as "the one who is in the world.")

Because the Spirit of the living God lives in you, you are a conqueror. You are filled with divine power that gives you strength far beyond the best that the enemy can muster up. You can destroy empty arguments in your head. You can have a totally renewed way of thinking. You can resist temptation. You are strong—not because of your innate fortitude, but because the Holy Spirit lives in you.

2. According to Ephesians 5:8, what were we once, and what are we now? How are we to live?

We can spend our entire lives in the shadowlands, never experiencing the life of Technicolor beauty we were created for. Lies masquerade as reality in the darkness. We don't see clearly. It's the enemy's playground, and he sows despair wherever there is agreement with lies. Hope grows dim, and we feel stuck in our circumstances. We doubt things will ever change. The pathway out of the shadowlands is covered with brambles and thorns, and we assume that moving through it will be unbearably painful.

God beckons us on a journey of healing, and yes, the pathway looks daunting. At the same time, the invitation to step into the light of who we truly are awakens in us the yearning for more.

How do we begin to move toward this light, this freedom? We wrestle. We go to the mat and grab hold of the lies to compare them to truth. We wrestle with empty arguments that make us doubt the trustworthiness of God. And this is a messy process. It doesn't feel good. At so many different points in the process, we want to quit and go back to what is comfortable. Yet something within us believes that going backward means we will never taste real healing and wholeness. We so want to be in control, yet at the same time, we are beginning to realize that no matter what we do, things will always be out of our hands. We hate this truth, and feel we are in a free fall. We wonder where and how it will end.

My precious friend, I know where it ends. I believe it with every fiber of my being. I would die for this truth—I believe it that completely. Here it is:

Underneath our free fall are *His everlasting arms.*

He catches us. He scoops us up and tells us we are beloved. He looks deep in our eyes and invites us, again, to trust Him.

If the Wrestling brings us to a place of childlike surrender to Jesus, then the Light of the World will illuminate the path in front of us so we can discover our destiny. True, it isn't like a landing strip that we can see for miles. He usually just shines on the next step. But that's all we need if we keep hold of His hand, because He always goes ahead of us.

And if we persevere, if we do not lose heart and give up, truth will win. If we do not let go, we will see that although the path is covered with thorns, Jesus goes before us and cuts away anything unbearable. There is suffering on the path to healing, but we receive the supernatural ability to keep walking. Jesus allows the sharpest thorns to pierce Him instead of us, and then ushers us into a place of wholeness and restoration. "By his wounds, you have been healed" (1 Peter 2:24).

3. According to the final two sentences of CCC 1695, who enlightens and strengthens us to live as "children of light" through "all that is good and right and true?" How does this happen?

4. A. The Holy Spirit heals the wounds of sin and renews us on the inside through a spiritual transformation (CCC 1695), but we need to cooperate with that work in order to live as children of light. What are we to do, according to Ephesians 5:10–13?

   B. Are there any "fruitless works of darkness" you are taking part in that you need to walk away from?

   C. Are there any fruitless works of darkness that you find especially disturbing? Is there some type of injustice that causes you to jump off the couch saying, "Something has got to be done about this"? What is one small step you could take to expose and push back the darkness?

Quiet your heart and enjoy His presence. . . . The light shines in the darkness and the darkness has not overcome it.

Often the darkness we are dealing with isn't outside us; it's coming from within. Our ability to look in the mirror and self-deceive is quite staggering. Being darkened in understanding (Ephesians 4:18) is caused by hardness of heart, which means we often have to ask God to soften our hearts so that we want to understand and see things as He does—in the light of truth.

Ephesians 5:14 challenges us to "awake, O sleeper, and arise from the dead, and Christ will give you light." Living as a child of the light means that we have become fully alive. It requires that we wake up from our slumber or our state of numbness and proactively follow Christ. Jesus explains this in John 8:12: "I am the light of the world. Whoever follows me will not walk in darkness, but will have the light of life."

When we are following Christ closely, we are all set to follow Saint Teresa of Calcutta's advice. She recommended that whenever someone says something hurtful to us, we immediately go to Jesus and ask Him if it's true. If it is, we should be thankful that light has been shed on one of our blind spots. If it isn't, then we can let it go and walk in freedom.

We are truly free to the extent that truth has entered our hearts. In order to really welcome truth, we have to purposefully walk into it. We have to search for it. We have to ask for it. We have to give trusted and truth-telling loved ones permission to speak it to us.

Dear Lord,

Please soften my heart. I know I should want to see myself fully, with all my weaknesses and strengths, but most days I feel like I am just fighting to keep my head above water. To proactively ask you or someone I love to shed light on one more area where I need to improve sounds absolutely miserable.

Yet I know you love me, and that you'll only show me what is necessary so that I can live with peace and joy. And I know that you are gentle. You promise in Isaiah 42:3 that you will not break a bruised reed or snuff out a smoldering wick. So help me to desire truth and light more than self-deception and darkness. Help me to have a little more courage than fear.

Help me to become a fearless truth seeker who isn't afraid of the light. May I confess quickly and then bask in the freedom of forgiveness. As Saint John Paul II said, "Darkness can only be scattered by light, and hatred can only be conquered by love."[25] So I invite your love to flood my heart and illuminate my soul. Amen.

---

[25] Saint John Paul II, "Address of His Holiness Pope John Paul II To the Diplomatic Corps" (speech, Vatican City, January 10, 2002), The Holy See, http://w2.vatican.va/content/john-paul-ii/en/speeches/2002/january/documents/hf_jp-ii_spe_20020110_diplomatic-corps.html.

Day Three
OPPORTUNITY

Read Ephesians 5:15–20.

1. List all the things we will and won't do if we are going to live as wise women, according to Ephesians 5:15–20.

   A. If we're going to live as wise women, we *will*:

   B. If we're going to live as wise women, we will *not*:

"Watch carefully then how you live" (Ephesians 5:15). In other words, your life of freedom is not just going to automatically blossom because you are wishing for it. It's going to come as you make the commitment to watch carefully how you are living.

Does this mean it's all up to you? No, God is at work within you. Philippians 2:13 (MSG) says, "That energy is *God's* energy, an energy deep within you, God himself willing and working at what will give him the most pleasure."

2. In verse 16, Saint Paul challenges us to make the most of the opportunity at hand. He acknowledges that we are surrounded by evil, and that its presence makes it hard to live the way God desires. But we are provided constant opportunities to build the spiritual muscles of self-discipline, trust, and faith. *These opportunities are the circumstances in our lives that we most want to change or get rid of.*

When life throws me a curveball, my first words to God are usually, "What on earth is going on? What are you doing?!" That's my knee-jerk reaction to shocking or painful situations. It's normal. But when I'm being wise, I move beyond reacting to responding. I settle down a bit and shift my perspective. When I follow Ephesians 5:16, I say, "I'm going to make the most of this opportunity. I hate this set of circumstances (Can I say that again? *I hate it.*), but here I am. I have no choice but to go through it, but it's up to me whether I come out the other end better or bitter."

Instead of shaking our fists at God and asking Him why He is asleep on the job, we can ask, "What are you trying to teach me here?" This is what Saint Paul is talking about in Ephesians 5:17 when he exhorts us to "not continue in ignorance but try to understand what is the will of the Lord."

Saint Ignatius has said that the enemy prowls around our souls, making a study of them. He looks for the weak points, and that's where he attacks. He wants to destroy us. But the very thing he intends for our destruction, God intends to use for good. That's why Saint Paul can refer to suffering as an "opportunity."

When the enemy jabs his sword into our hearts through suffering, when he hits on an old wound that we thought was long buried or a fresh one is created, he thinks he's victorious. And God, with all His goodness and power, looks at the enemy and says, "Thank you very much. What you intended to destroy in her has now allowed her to awaken to an area of her heart that I have been waiting to heal. I needed her to notice it, and now I'm waiting to see if she makes the most of this opportunity and invites me into the pain."

And this is exactly when we most want to run. This is when we want to numb ourselves to any negative emotion or experience. But if we will resist the urge, if we will lean into the pain and name it, if we will start to explore the lies that are swirling in our heads, God will be able to reach in, speak truth, and heal.

A. Is there an area of your life where you are experiencing suffering? How are you responding to it? Are you angry with God? Are you afraid? Are you questioning His goodness? Be honest. He already knows. He wants to hear how you really feel.

B. I know this is an area of pain. But I'm going to step into that sacred ground of suffering and echo Jesus' words to the paralyzed man: "Do you want to get well?" Do you want the healing and freedom that can come on the other side of this suffering?

3. A. What does Ephesians 5:18 tell us to avoid? As you reflect on what we have learned about the temptation to numb ourselves, can you apply this verse to your own life? Have you used alcohol to numb pain? What does this verse suggest is an alternative choice?

Wine gives us a temporary high and allows us to numb out. We don't feel the hard circumstances so acutely, and that can be a welcome retreat. It can also dull our conscience, leading to choices we later regret. In the very moment when we might have had a real breakthrough in healing, alcohol can offer a cheap substitute. It's worth remembering that in addition to not solving our problems, alcohol is a depressant. What goes up must come down.

Wouldn't you rather be filled with something that brings you lasting joy? Alcohol might give us a temporary high, but being filled with the Holy Spirit brings a depth of fulfillment and peace that steadies and strengthens us.

B. The Holy Spirit is given to us in baptism (CCC 784) and confirmation (CCC 1302). In the words of Sister Ann Shields, "God did not leave us orphaned; he assured us that he would send us his Spirit . . . the seed is given in Baptism . . . but we must be willing to cooperate and, once we reach the age of reason, to choose more and more to conform our lives to him."[26] The seed is planted in baptism, and then grows deeper roots in confirmation. According to CCC 1303, "Confirmation brings an increase and a deepening of baptismal grace." It roots us more firmly in our identity as beloved daughters of God, unites us to Jesus, increases the gifts of the Holy Spirit in us, strengthens our bond to the Church, and gives us special strength from the Holy Spirit. That is what is on offer to us every minute of every day.

What do we learn about the Holy Spirit from the following verses?

John 14:15–18, 26

---

[26] Sister Ann Shields, SGL, *More of the Holy Spirit: How to Keep the Fire Burning in Our Hearts* (Frederick, MD: The Word Among Us, 2013), 18–19.

Romans 8:26

Acts 1:8

2 Corinthians 3:17

The Holy Spirit leads us to freedom by leading us into truth. When we are filled with the Holy Spirit, He helps us wrestle with the lies that mess with us. He faithfully brings God's truth to our minds so we can grasp hold of it instead. He knows where we are weak and wounded, reaches into those deep places, and heals us.

We read in John 14:26 that the Holy Spirit will remind us of everything Jesus taught. One of the most important things Jesus said is, "Behold, I am with you always, until the end of the age" (Matthew 28:20). When we recognize our places of woundedness and hurt, we often go back to memories and wonder where Jesus was. Did He abandon us? Did He reject us? The Holy Spirit responds to these questions with an emphatic *no*. Jesus promised to be with us always. He has never left us. Healing comes to our hearts when we realize that in the very moments that we felt the most alone, Jesus was there. As we open ourselves to the ministry of the Holy Spirit, He helps us to explore this truth in a personal, transformative way.

4. How can we be filled with the Holy Spirit? See Luke 11:13.

The graces of the Holy Spirit are given to us in baptism and confirmation, but at some point, we need to make an adult decision to embrace them—to *receive* them—if we want to be filled with the Holy Spirit. This is not something that automatically happens because we went through the motions. We need to make a personal decision to ask the Holy Spirit to fill us.

Quiet your heart and enjoy His presence. . . . May the Holy Spirit surround and fill you.

Experiencing a filling of the Holy Spirit is connected to our openness and our obedience. Are you willing to open your heart to Him in prayer and invite Him in? If so, I encourage you to slowly and thoughtfully pray the following:

Come, Holy Spirit. I invite you to fill me. There is no place within me that I am holding back from you. Go where you will, and in each place, bring healing, wisdom, truth, and wholeness. I want you and all that you have for me. I ask you to be at the center of my life. My hands are open to receive you and all your gifts.

Come, Holy Spirit. I ask you to activate the gifts that you placed within me in baptism and confirmation. Help me to proactively open them by recognizing that they were given to me, personally, to empower me and make me more like Jesus. Please make those gifts alive in me.

Come, Holy Spirit. Give me the strength to obey. I know that when I ignore your nudges and do whatever I feel like doing, I diminish your power in my life.

Come, Holy Spirit. There is a throne in my heart. We can't both sit on the throne. So I am inviting you to take your rightful place within me, and I kneel before you with openness and obedience. Amen.

Day Four
MUTUAL SUBMISSION

This day's Scripture passage contains some hot-button words and verses that are easily misunderstood. We're going to dive into the deeper meanings so we don't miss out on truths that can truly transform our closest relationships. Saint Paul directs the bulk of these words to husbands and wives, but the application found here can be much broader. So if you are single, don't skip these passages. The call to selfless living that disarms a skeptical world issues a challenge to each and every one of God's beloved daughters.

Our closest relationships carry the potential for the greatest highs (feeling cherished, chosen, and safe) and the deepest lows (feeling betrayed, devalued, and alone). Just about every other emotion in between can be felt as well. In marriage relationships, we rub up against each other the closest, and so the friction felt is going to be acute. Those of us who are married will experience many of our best opportunities to grow more like Christ within the chafing of that relationship.

God's desire is for us to experience marriage as a wellspring of love within the family. This would provide a source of security for everyone, as we would be rooted and grounded in love (Ephesians 3:17). But when this is not what we experience, insecurity results, which leads to fear. When fear reigns, we find it hard to trust, and turn to self-protective coping mechanisms. The only way we can continue to love in the midst of these unideal circumstances is to cling to the following belief: Even when people betray us and fall short of what we need, God always remains faithful (2 Timothy 2:13). We ask that His perfect love cast out our fear (1 John 4:18).

The passage of Scripture we're going to study today pitches a vision for what marriage can be. Reading it might fill you with longing, irritation, or even the desire to throw this book across the room if your marriage has been an area of real struggle.

Hang in there as we unpack these verses. Don't get stuck on words until you take the time with me to discover their real meaning. We're going to wrestle with verses that have aggravated women for decades, and we are going to glean the goodness contained for us in them.

Read Ephesians 5:21–33.

1. Who is to be subordinate and to whom, according to Ephesians 5:21? Why?

This passage is giving us a code of conduct for relating to one another and describes a *mutual* submission. What additional insights do we gain from the following verses in terms of what this looks like in day-to-day life?

1 Corinthians 13:5

Galatians 5:13

Philippians 2:3–4

The phrase "be subordinate" comes from the Greek verb *hypotasso*, which means "to place or arrange under."[27] This is a choice we make—not because we are less than or doormats, but because being subordinate to one another in love means we regard others as more important than ourselves. At the other end of the spectrum we find narcissism.

We're told to serve one another in love. So we look at what the people around us need, and *we do what we can to arrange ourselves to be a support under those people.* When I picture this, it reminds me of the story of an Old Testament battle found in Exodus 17:8–13:

> Then Amalek came and waged war against Israel in Rephidim. Moses said to Joshua, "Choose some men for us, and tomorrow go out and engage Amalek in battle. I will be standing on top of the hill with the staff of God in my hand." Joshua did as Moses told him; he engaged Amalek in battle while Moses, Aaron and Hur climbed to the top of the hill. As long as Moses kept his hands raised up, Israel had the better of the fight, but when he let his hands rest, Amalek had the better of the fight. Moses' hands, however, grew tired; so they took a rock and put it under him and he sat on it. Meanwhile Aaron and Hur supported his hands, one on one side and one on the other, so that his hands remained steady until sunset. And Joshua defeated Amalek.

There is nothing degrading about choosing to take your eyes off yourself and focus on the needs of others. Aaron and Hur were no less important than Moses in the battle. The victory came when everyone kept their eyes on the main thing they all were after: freedom.

2. What do we learn from Ephesians 5:22–24 about how a wife is to relate to her husband?

Deep breath, ladies. I know that reading this makes us uncomfortable. Submitting our will to someone else does not come easy. Being told we *should do* anything makes most of us want to grab hold of something we think we can control. Let's resist that urge and press deeper into why Saint Paul gave us these instructions.

---

[27] Williamson, *Ephesians*, 155.

3. What instructions did Saint Paul give husbands about how they are to treat their wives? See Ephesians 5:24–28.

Knowing that we would struggle with this passage, Saint John Paul II devoted his Wednesday audiences from July 28 to December 15, 1982, to these verses and unpacked them more in his *Theology of the Body* and his apostolic letter *On the Dignity and Vocation of Women*. The following excerpts from his writing give a beautiful perspective for us:

> The husband is above all, he who loves and the wife, on the other hand is she who is loved. One could even hazard the idea that the wife's submission to her husband, understood in the context of the entire passage of Ephesians, signifies above all the "experiencing of love." This is all the more so since this submission is related to the image of the submission of the Church to Christ, which certainly consists in experiencing his love.[28]

> [The] essence of the love of a husband is to lay down his life for his bride.[29]

> [This kind of] love excludes every kind of submission by which the wife would become a servant or slave of the husband, an object of one-sided submission. Love makes the husband simultaneously subject to the wife, and subject in this to the Lord himself, as the wife is to the husband.[30, 31]

I could delve into commentaries and unpack other insights into what all of this means. But instead, I just want to share what I have found to be true, personally. *This is what works.* When I stop analyzing and focusing on my rights, when I simply look at my marriage from this perspective, things begin to change for the better. The way I see it, God has asked my husband to be the head of our family, just as He asked Moses to lead the Israelites. There are many moments when Moses and my husband have wished that someone else was carrying that responsibility. Yes, there are times when it's awesome to be in charge, but more often, leading simply means sacrificing. It means hard work. It means carrying burdens that others don't have to carry.

---

[28] Saint John Paul II, *General Audience: Theology of the Body: Sacredness of the Human Body and Marriage*, September 1, 1982.

[29] Saint John Paul II, *General Audience: Theology of the Body: Reverence for Christ the Basis of Relationship Between Spouses*, August 11, 1982.

[30] Saint John Paul II, *Apostolic Letter: Mulieris Dignitatem: On the Dignity and Vocation of Women*, August 15, 1988, 29.

[31] Schuchts, *Healing the Whole Person Workbook*, 22.

Leo stands at the head of our family, and he takes the brunt of the battle before it hits us. He carries our concerns and needs, and I know he gets weary. Is it too much for me to go find him a rock to sit on? To arrange myself beneath him and hold up his arms at those times? Or is it actually an enormous privilege? Which perspective I choose is up to me.

I have found that when I stop grasping for control, my husband feels respected. He tends to respond to me with sacrificial love. Here are some game-changing questions and comments:

"How can I support you today?"

"I trust you."

"You make good decisions."

"I believe in you."

"You are strong and I respect you."

It's a tough and tenacious woman who can set aside her rights and desires to look to the needs of another. It takes tremendous self-control to choose words wisely instead of lashing out emotionally. This is a woman who has taken seriously the command to "Be imitators of God" (Ephesians 5:1). After all, this is how Jesus lived.

4. There is something big that God is trying to communicate to the world through the sacrament of marriage. When we are able to live out the principles of Ephesians 5, an onlooking world gets a glimpse of what Christ's love for the Church is like. Because of this, you can be assured that the enemy will do all he can to divide and conquer within a marriage. This means that he will exploit our wounds, and tempt us to see our spouse as the real enemy.

Because this is the relationship closest to you, your husband will often trigger your deepest wounds. All too often we falsely believe that the battle is between the husband and wife. The truth is, the enemy is behind our tendency to fill in the gaps, attributing ill motive when there often is none.

If you are married, do you believe you see the best in your husband, or are you apt to attribute to him the worst possible motive? Are there any areas of your marriage where you need to grow in your willingness to support and serve your husband? When you see each other at the end of the day, what does he see reflected in your face—excitement, irritation, disappointment? Food for thought: You are his mirror—a powerful reflector of his worth.

If you are not married, is there another close relationship in which you are finding it difficult to put another's needs before your own? Is there something practical you can do to serve him or her in love? Whose arms are getting weary? Can you come under them and offer support?

Quiet your heart and enjoy His presence. . . . God is your helper and sustainer.

Back in Genesis, Eve was given to Adam as his "helper," or ezer kenegdo *in Hebrew, and most women have been annoyed by this role ever since. We interpret the word to mean "less than" or "subservient." But if we dig deeper into the meaning of* ezer kenegdo, *we'll gain a critical perspective regarding the dignity inherent in that word. There are twenty other places in the Bible where this phrase is used, and in every case, it is used to describe God. It's the word used to illustrate Him sweeping in and saving us when we are most desperate.*

One way we can fulfill the role of helper is by being mature enough to look beyond the most obvious facts in a conflict to see what is going on underneath. Everything changes when we recognize that hurting people hurt people. Even if our spouse isn't open to us helping him to see the deeper issues or wounds that are being triggered, our relationship is helped when we see it. This allows us to whisper to ourselves, "This isn't about what it's about." There is something more. There is something deeper. We help the situation when we ask questions and seek to understand rather than to immediately judge.

Dear Lord,

I wish my natural inclination was to serve and support, but the truth is, I wrestle with this. If it were just in the context of human relationships, that would be one thing. But I see this struggle in my relationship with you, too. I want my own way, I want the easy way, and I want to be at the center. Forgive me. Help me to see that if I grow in trust of you, I'll find it far easier to step in and serve, leaving the results to you. Please increase my faith and trust in you. May I see you as my ezer kenegdo—*my sustainer, my Savior, my help. Please come and heal my heart. Restore and rebuild what has been shattered within me.*

I haven't always been loved very well. This has left wounds that make self-protection so appealing to me. But I can't self-protect and love at the same time. Help me to have healthy boundaries, but may they not be so tight that there is no room for me to come under someone's weary arms to offer support. May I remember that even as I hold up the arms of the one I love, you are underneath me, providing me with the help and support that I need. Please heal my wounds and increase my trust. Amen.

"The eternal God is your refuge, and underneath are the everlasting arms." (Deuteronomy 33:27)

Day Five
ROOTS

Read Ephesians 6:1–4.

It has been said that pain that is not transformed is transmitted to others. We may *think* we have dealt with our wounds by covering them with busyness and productivity. We may have a "mind over matter" mentality that ignores what's going on underneath, but pain has a way of seeping out despite our best attempts to stop it.

Because of this, your parents likely carried their own unhealed wounds into your family. There probably was some baggage. The result? Imperfect, hurting parents end up inadvertently hurting their children.

Author Peggy O'Mara has written that the way we talk to our children becomes their inner voice. Vows, lies, and hurts can be passed down from one generation to the next. The critical voice of an earthly parent can drown out the gentle voice of our heavenly Father. He has never stopped calling you beloved, but any opposing voice needs to be quieted so that you can hear His words of blessing and acceptance.

I promise you, generational strongholds can be broken. You can be the first to create a new legacy—to write a different ending to the story. By God's grace, you can go down to the roots and dig out what has harmed you. It is possible to continue to honor your family of origin and take an honest look at ways you were wounded in childhood. We can cling to hope that things do not need to end as they have begun.

As we look at Saint Paul's instructions for the family, may we remember that God promises to restore the years the locusts have eaten (Joel 2:25). He will redeem the mess. We can echo the words of the psalmist in Psalm 27:13: "I would have lost heart, unless I had believed that I would see the goodness of the Lord in the land of the living." It may seem like we are only making things worse when we look back on ways we were hurt in childhood. But God promises that as wounds are lifted up to Him, He will heal them. Nothing will be wasted. Nothing is beyond the reach of His healing hand. He can reach the roots, the deepest places, and bring restoration.

1. A. What are the instructions given to children in Ephesians 6:1–2?

   While we are to obey our parents when we are children, we are to honor them when we are adults. There comes a point when we are not under an obligation to do things our parents' way or live entirely according to their desires.

   B. What are we commanded to do in Ephesians 5:31?

   The phrase used to describe this process is "leave and cleave." This can be difficult to do. Our upbringing has hardwired us in certain ways. Vows we have made to self-protect may be ones that our family of origin has wanted us to keep. Many of us have been taught that family secrets are not meant to be shared, that to bring them up will bring shame on the family. This can lead to a lot of confusion as we seek to make sense of childhood wounds.

   It is possible to honor our parents—to respect and treat them with dignity—while being honest about things that have hurt us. If we refuse to do this—if we equate honest reflection with family betrayal or dishonor—we will forfeit healing. We can only be healed in areas that we know and acknowledge need the Great Physician's touch.

   C. Reflect on your "inner voice." How do you talk to yourself? Are you as tender with yourself as you are with others? Can you see any indication that your inner voice is similar to the way you were spoken to as a child by your parents?

   D. Is there something from your childhood that you would like God to heal? What are some of the family secrets you have carried in shame that have become weights around your neck? What might it feel like to offer those to God?

2. Ephesians 6:4 tells fathers (and mothers) not to provoke their children to anger. List some ways this might happen in a family.

When the basic need of a child for love, security, and acceptance is not met by a parent, the child will look for those things in other places. This will often lead the child to root herself in ungodly self-reliance. The alternative is to go to God to have needs met, but it's difficult for a child to understand how to do that when it is not modeled for her. Ungodly self-reliance leads all of us to sin, because we are looking for something other than God to satisfy us. We are saying (whether we realize it or not), "I'm going to fix this problem because I can't trust that God will meet me here." Instead of waiting for God to show up, we want the pain to go away as quickly as possible. Can you see this pattern in your adult life? I know I certainly can. Recognizing that this is where my behavior naturally leads me reminds me that it's incredibly difficult for a child to navigate this. In a child's need to feel secure, she will adopt coping mechanisms that are often rooted in self-reliance. This is a survival instinct. But as a child grows, it's important to recognize that what helped her survive in childhood is now working against her. Healing is needed if she is going to walk in freedom.

One of the sins that can result from ungodly self-reliance is anger. Dr. Bob Schuchts identifies common manifestations of anger as follows: self-righteousness, judgment, bitterness, resentment, depression, passive-aggressive behavior, rage, revenge, retaliation, murder, violence, malice, verbal abuse, insults, and slander.

When we really struggle with anger, we idolize control and power. We wrongly believe that these things will help us to gain love, security, and acceptance. This is a pattern that can take root in childhood and carry into adulthood.

We make the mistake of looking at the manifestations of anger (or any sin) and trying to get rid of them. But if we really want to experience freedom, we need to get down to the root. We need to work backward until we find the moment when we first grabbed hold of self-reliance (likely through power and control). The way we begin to unpack this is by reflecting on our earliest memory of a strong emotion of anger.

Do you see examples in your life when you were provoked to anger, shame, hatred, self-contempt, or fear in a significant way? If so, share the memory here.

It is absolutely critical that you recognize that in those very moments when you were provoked to anger, or driven to fear, or felt abandoned, or experienced rejection, or were covered in shame, or felt utterly out of control, or were confused or powerless, *God was there.* He did not leave you. His love was not taken from you. You were never out of His sight or out of His grasp. I know this might feel so hard to believe. I completely understand if this doesn't feel true. But whether something *feels* true does not determine whether it *is* true. You may need someone gifted in the ministry of healing to help you process and pray through this. Seek this help. Ask God to lead you to someone who can guide you in this way.

But for now, I promise you, *He was there.* And His presence then, and now, makes all the difference. And I acknowledge that recognizing His presence might also lead to anger. Because if He was there, then why didn't He do something to stop whatever happened to you? This emotion is not something to be skipped over or pushed away. If this is where you are, I encourage you to find a trusted counselor or mentor to work through these valid emotions.

3. No one loves perfectly—not our parents, and not us. Thankfully, God steps in and fills in the gaps. Read the following verses and record your thoughts on how He does that.

   Psalm 68:6 (NAB)

   Romans 8:35–39

   Philippians 4:19

You may look back at your childhood and have difficulty seeing God's presence. I understand that. The truth is, God shows up in our lives in thousands of ways, and we only perceive a few of them. It's not that He isn't there. It's not that He isn't intervening and providing. We just can't see the evidence, and so we assume He is absent. It's been said that fear is **F**alse **E**vidence **A**ppearing **R**eal. When we think we are alone, fear is a natural response. It leads to self-protection and self-reliance. We need to fill our minds with truth so that we can combat the lies suggesting that God left us when we most needed Him. The truth? Nothing can or has ever separated us from His love.

4. Read Ephesians 6:5–9. These are Saint Paul's instructions to slaves and masters. Reading this might make you wonder if Paul is suggesting that slavery is a good thing. Nothing could be further from the truth. According to theologian N. T. Wright, "Paul could no more envisage a world without slavery than we can envisage a world without electricity . . . Paul wasn't attempting to design a new way for the world to run."[32] That being said, his instructions were revolutionary. In telling the masters that in God's eyes, everyone was equal—that they were to treat their slaves with goodness and sincerity, seeking God's will at all times—he was issuing a countercultural challenge.

"One of my favorite verses is tucked into the middle of this passage. Ephesians 6:6-8 says that we are to do "the will of God from the heart, rendering service with a good will as to the Lord and not to men, knowing that whatever good any one does, he will receive the same again from the Lord."

This verse challenges me to look past the person I am called to serve and to fix my eyes on Christ. When I don't feel like serving someone, when I feel that he or she doesn't deserve it, I look past the person and do the act of service for Jesus.

Is there someone God is calling you to serve who you don't feel deserves it? Can you do that act of service for Christ instead? What additional insight do you gain from Matthew 25:40?

Quiet your heart and enjoy His presence. . . . You are rooted in His love.

This remains Saint Paul's prayer for you:

"That you, rooted and grounded in love, may have strength to comprehend with all the holy ones what is the breadth and length and height and depth [of the] love of Christ." (Ephesians 3:17–18)

When you know that you are rooted and grounded in the love of Christ, you don't have to prove your worth. Serving doesn't affect your status—you recognize that you are already elevated to the honored position of daughter of the King of the universe.

When you know that you are rooted and grounded in the love of Christ, you are able to forgive your parents for the ways they loved you imperfectly.

---

[32] N. T. Wright, *Paul for Everyone: The Prison Letters* (Louisville, KY: Westminster John Knox Press, 2004), 70.

When you know that you are rooted and grounded in the love of Christ, you are able to forgive yourself for the ways you love imperfectly.

When you know that you are rooted and grounded in the love of Christ, you are able to ask Him to accompany you through painful memories and ask Him to heal you in those tender, sacred places.

Jesus issues you an invitation into the most intimate and passionate of love relationships. No man can love you the way He does. He is utterly faithful, steadfast, unchanging, tender, understanding, and strong. He is the Lion of Judah, who will sweep in and fight for you. Let Him be your rescuer.

"The Lord will fight for you. You need only to be still." (Exodus 14:14)

Conclusion

*"We are not the sum of our weaknesses and failures. We are the sum of the Father's love for us." —
Saint John Paul II*

You are beloved. You are the pearl of greatest price. You were worth everything to Jesus—even more than His life. He is passionate about you.

He is a warrior. Your rescuer and lover is not passive. He doesn't just indifferently watch as the enemy tries to rob you of your inheritance as a daughter of the King.

When Jesus sees you flirt with the darkness, He rushes in to shed light.

When Jesus sees your choices lead you down a dangerous path, He allows you to feel discomfort to draw you back to Him.

When Jesus sees you getting sleepy and complacent, He wakes you up. Sometimes it isn't very gentle, but it's always for your good.

When Jesus sees you reach for the glass of wine instead of reaching out for Him, He waits, knowing it won't really satisfy you.

When Jesus sees you hurt in the closest of relationships, He catches you as you crumble and cradles you in His arms.

When Jesus sees you stepping out to serve and knows you don't feel able, He whispers, "Do it for me instead. I see you. I see your sacrifice. It matters."

Does something in your heart want to ask Him to prove this? Do doubts linger and make you wonder if it all is too good to be true?

My dear friend, He already has proven these words to be true. That's what He was doing on the cross. He stretched out His arms and said, "This. This is how much I love you. Not just to the moon and back. To the depths of hell and back. There is nowhere I will not go and fight for you."

Open your heart to the only One who can totally be trusted with the most vulnerable part of you. He will not fail you.

My Resolution

In what specific way will I apply what I have learned in this lesson?

Examples:

1. I have been playing around in the darkness with a particular sin: _____ (list it here). I want to walk in the light. I commit to going to confession and then doing all I can to eradicate this sin. I will flee from it. I commit to no longer playing around with it. I will call it what God calls it and stop justifying my behavior.

2. I am finding it very difficult to serve and support _____ (list the person). Instead of trying to drum up motivation or desire to serve him or her, I will do it for Jesus. I will consider it my service to Him instead.

3. I have identified some wounds from my childhood, and I struggle to see that Jesus was with me there. I will ask God to lead me to someone who can help me pray and work through this.

My resolution:

Catechism Clips

CCC 784 On entering the People of God through faith and Baptism, one receives a share in this people's unique, *priestly* vocation: "Christ the Lord, high priest taken from among men, has made this new people 'a kingdom of priests to God, his Father.' The baptized, by regeneration and the anointing of the Holy Spirit, are *consecrated* to be a spiritual house and a holy priesthood."

CCC 1302 It is evident from its celebration that the effect of the sacrament of Confirmation is the special outpouring of the Holy Spirit as once granted to the apostles on the day of Pentecost.

CCC 1303 From this fact, Confirmation brings an increase and deepening of baptismal grace:

- it roots us more deeply in the divine filiation which makes us cry, "Abba! Father!";
- it unites us more firmly to Christ;
- it increases the gifts of the Holy Spirit in us;
- it renders our bond with the Church more perfect;
- it gives us a special strength of the Holy Spirit to spread and defend the faith by word and action as true witnesses of Christ, to confess the name of Christ boldly, and never to be ashamed of the Cross:

> Recall then that you have received the spiritual seal, the spirit of wisdom and understanding, the spirit of right judgment and courage, the spirit of knowledge and reverence, the spirit of holy fear in God's presence. Guard what you have received. God the Father has marked you with his sign; Christ the Lord has confirmed you and has placed his pledge, the Spirit, in your hearts.

CCC 1695 "Justified in the name of the Lord Jesus Christ and in the Spirit of our God," "sanctified . . . [and] called to be saints," Christians have become the temple of the *Holy Spirit*. This "Spirit of the Son" teaches them to pray to the Father and, having become their life, prompts them to act so as to bear "the fruit of the Spirit" by charity in action. **Healing the wounds of sin, the Holy Spirit renews us interiorly through a spiritual transformation. He enlightens and strengthens us to live as "children of light" through "all that is good and right and true."**

we fall into sin so we avoid suffering

our tears are sacred to God

Lesson 9

PASSIONATE TALK

Accompanying talk can be viewed by DVD or digital download purchase or access online at walkingwithpurpose.com/videos.

"Women who have WAKENED, who are willing to WRESTLE, are women who are ready to be WARRIORS. And the coward quakes at the thought of all of us armed with truth, strengthened by the knowledge of our true identity, stepping out to reclaim territory he thought was his."

I. The Gift of Being Stripped Down

The enemy knows our __wounds__ and __exploits__ them.

But when we courageously invite Jesus into the mess and pain, He __redeems__ it and brings __healing__.

II. How to Suffer Redemptively

A. Recognizing our Woundedness

"What really hurts is not so much suffering itself as the fear of suffering. If welcomed trustingly and peacefully, suffering makes us grow. It matures and trains us, purifies us, teaches us how to love unselfishly, makes us poor in heart, humble, gentle, and compassionate toward our neighbor. Fear of suffering, on the other hand, hardens us in self-protective, defensive attitudes, and often leads us to make irrational choices with disastrous consequences.[33] —Father Jacques Philippe

B. Following Jesus' Example

---

[33] Jacques Philippe, *Interior Freedom* (New York: Scepter Publishing 2002), 47.

III. St. Ignatius' Practical Tips from Discernment of Spirits[34]

    A. Get a Grip on Your Thoughts

        i. Be Aware
        ii. Understand
        iii. Take Action

    B. Stay the Course

    C. Charge Forward and Do More

Discussion Questions

1. We heard in the talk that "suffering that is not transformed is transmitted." Share an example from your own life or the life of someone you know of suffering being transformed.

2. Saint Ignatius' discernment of spirits gives us three things we can do in the midst of suffering: get a grip on our thoughts, stay the course, and charge forward and do more. When you are suffering, which of the three do you find hardest to do?

3. In which area of your life are you facing the choice of either shaking your fist at God or offering Him the surrender of your will—your FIAT?

God uses everything

---

[34] For a great explanation of St. Ignatius' Discernment of Spirits, I recommend the following book: Timothy M. Gallagher, *Discernment of Spirits: An Ignatian Guide for Everyday Living* (New York: Crossroad Publishing Company, 2005).

THE Warrior

RECLAIMING GROUND & MOVING FORWARD

 NOTES

Lesson 10

BRAVE BIBLE STUDY

Introduction

"We have been called to heal wounds, to unite what has fallen apart, and to bring home those who have lost their way." —Saint Francis of Assisi

Warriors, it's time to arise.

We have **wakened** to our true identity, and know that the enemy wants to steal all that we have inherited as God's beloved daughters.

We have begun to **wrestle** with the lies and truth in our minds, and to battle through the hard work of maturing and taking our thoughts captive to Christ.

We'll never feel entirely ready to be **warriors**, but my friends, it's time.

There is a whole world out there that desperately needs strong women who aren't just taking care of themselves. Look around. People we love are struggling on all sides. It's time to rise from our seats on the sidelines and engage the battle offensively. I know you don't have all the answers, but what you have is enough. The Holy Spirit dwells within you, and He will give you all that is needed to get out there and take back territory that the enemy has claimed.

"It's all up to me" is a lie. But so is "I can't do anything about this." Your yes to God—your fiat—is so important. The point isn't how much you are doing. It's whether you have decided to step into the battle, to make a difference in whatever way you can. Victory is achieved when one small yes to God is followed by another small yes. Bit by bit, we move forward.

Now is not the time to shrink back. Let's press on, allowing the saints to lead the way with their example. They didn't settle for comfort. Instead, they *lived* on the battlefield. They spoke frankly about the enemy, but never with the attitude of a defcatist. Saint Teresa of Ávila, a true Warrior, describes our reality well:

> These cursed spirits torment me quite frequently, but they do not frighten me in the least. For I am convinced that they cannot move except by God's permission. Let this be known well: every time we make the demons the object of our contempt, they lose their strength, and the soul acquires a greater superiority over them. They have no power except against cowardly souls who surrender their weapons.[35]

My friend, *never* surrender your weapons—especially the weapon of humility.

Does it surprise you to hear of that virtue described as a weapon? It truly is. In Philippians 2:3–11, Saint Paul teaches that it was through the humility of Jesus that the devil was defeated. Your awareness of your weaknesses, wounds, imperfections, and failures is actually one of your greatest strengths. As Saint John Climacus said, "Humility is the only virtue no demon can imitate."[36] Humility means that you see yourself as God sees you—no more and no less. Throughout *Fearless and Free*, you've been given the opportunity to pick up the mirror and look at yourself honestly. That hasn't always been easy. But I pray you have grown in awareness of your weaknesses, your wounds, and your imperfections because therein lies one of your greatest strengths. This is one of the ways we grow in humility. When you know you are weak, you are far more likely to lean on the Lord. God's power is made perfect in our weakness (2 Corinthians 12:9), but only if we ask Him to help us. Humility keeps us aware of our neediness. Despite our woundedness, we are not powerless, because we serve an all-powerful Savior. Despite our brokenness, we are not hopeless, because our God is making all things new and is always at work.

God has given us supernatural weapons for the battle. This lesson is all about learning what they are and how to wield them. Let's suit up and step out. Beloved, let's be brave daughters and Warriors. The battle is fierce, but victory is guaranteed.

"You draw near this day to battle against your enemies: Let not your heart faint; do not fear, or tremble, or be in dread of them; for the LORD your God is He that goes with you, to fight for you against your enemies, to give you the victory." (Deuteronomy 20:3–4)

---

[35] Thigpen, *Manual for Spiritual Warfare*, (Charlotte, NC: TAN Books, 2014), 147.
[36] Paul Thigpen, *Manual for Spiritual Warfare*, 143.

Day One
STAND FIRM

Read Ephesians 6:10–12.

1. From where are we to draw our strength, according to Ephesians 6:10? What alternative sources of strength do we often turn to instead?

2. A. According to Ephesians 6:11, why are we told to put on the armor of God?

   We put on the armor of God so that . . .

   Our job is to stand firm. God's job is to defeat the enemy. According to theologian Peter Williamson, "Defeating Satan is God's work and has been accomplished through the death and resurrection of Christ. Our first concern must be to defend the territory that Christ has won in our lives."[37]

   B. One of the best ways we can defend the territory Christ has won for us is to waken to what we are protecting and to the enemy's tactics. **We are protecting our true identity as beloved daughters of God, and the life purpose that God has for each one of us.** The enemy wants to steal both of those things so that we live defeated and unfulfilled lives. We are called to stand firm against his attacks, not letting his lies take us down. They fly at us, and we parry them with truth. We've spent a lot of time studying this tactic of attack with lies. What are some of his other tactics?

   According to Saint Ignatius' discernment of spirits, we have to be able to recognize "the fundamental direction of that person's spiritual life"[38] in order to identify what the enemy is up to and which tactic he is likely using. If a person is making choices that move her away from God, then the enemy is going to do all he can to keep her comfortable and focused on pleasures. He'll work on the imagination, causing the person to imagine all sorts of pleasant and enticing things that will be experienced if she sins. The enemy leads the

---

[37] Williamson, *Ephesians*, 191.
[38] Gallagher, *The Discernment of Spirits*, 31.

person to imagine that the thrill or pleasure will be worth it. God's tactic in that person's life will be very different. When someone's general direction is moving away from God, then He will do "precisely the opposite, 'stinging and biting,' arousing a sense of trouble in them and awakening them of their need for spiritual renewal and for God."[39] This is actually a kind and loving thing for God to do—allowing one to be hurt in order to heal.

When the fundamental direction of a person's life is toward God, then the enemy's tactic is to "bite, sadden, place obstacles, and disquiet with false reasons."[40]

Read the following definitions of the enemy's tactics from Father Timothy Gallagher's research on discernment of spirits, and share specific times you have experienced this in your own life in the midst of suffering or spiritual attack.

A biting that unsettles: "a biting, gnawing action that triggers a sense of anxiety, diminishing their peace, and undermining their delight in God's service."[41] In my life, I experience this as an anxious thought or worry that nips at my heart and shakes me up.

Sadness: "We find ourselves sad without knowing why. We cannot pray with devotion, nor contemplate, nor even speak or hear of the things of God with any interior taste or relish."[42] —Saint Ignatius of Loyola

Obstacles: "She begins to see the difficulties involved [in spiritual growth], the problems she will encounter if she continues to seek this spiritual growth. She is led to consider her own weakness. Increasingly she feels that she is too weak to overcome the obstacles, that this spiritual newness, though attractive in itself, is not attainable for her. The enemy places obstacles in her path so that she may not go forward."[43]

---

[39] Ibid., 36.
[40] Ibid, 38.
[41] Ibid, 40.
[42] Ibid., 40.
[43] Ibid, 41.

Disquiet with false reasons: This is a key way the enemy undermines our peace. He causes us to second-guess our spiritual progress and the truths we have learned about God and ourselves. We experience a general feeling of disquiet and unsettledness, and try to figure out why. The enemy suggests that it must be because all of this spiritual stuff is fake, or not meant for you, or other nonsense.

In the face of these tactics, we are to stand firm. We are able to do this by being aware of what is really going on, understanding who is at work behind the scenes, and then rejecting the lies that have been fed to us.

The enemy's tactics come at us like waves. Sometimes they are so strong we feel they are ripping through our mind and heart. But if we stand firm, they will eventually subside. They will gently wash over us. We will not indefinitely be swirling in that water. It will pass.

3. We *can* stand firm because the enemy is not the only one with tactics. God is also at work here. When we are under siege, God is at work consoling, strengthening, inspiring, and removing obstacles. "Behold, the guardian of Israel neither slumbers nor sleeps. The LORD is your guardian; the LORD is your shade at your right hand. . . . The LORD will guard you from all evil; he will guard your soul. The LORD will guard your coming and going both now and forever" (Psalm 121:4–8).

In what way have you seen evidence of God consoling, strengthening, and inspiring you? Have you experienced Him removing obstacles from your path? List them after the following definitions.

God consoles. One of the ways God consoles us is by sending a torrent of tears. Releasing them can bring a great deal of relief. Some of us need permission to cry a lifetime of tears. God gives you that permission. Rest in His embrace as you cry.

God strengthens. The indwelling Holy Spirit is real and present within you. You can call on Him to fill you with strength. This isn't a onetime thing. (I find that I need to ask for this daily, and sometimes moment by moment.) He will never fail to come through for you.

God inspires. His inspiration comes in various ways. Sometimes it's a little nudge we feel to look a bit longer at the beautiful sunset and remember that He made beauty to bring us delight. Perhaps He's led you to a particular passage of Scripture, a book, or a song that has brought inspiration and comfort. Often He inspires us by speaking to us through people. The true source of all that is good is God.

God removes obstacles. In the same way that God parted the Red Sea so the Israelites could walk over dry ground to freedom, He clears the way for us. He creates opportunities for important conversations and softens hearts so they can receive what we say. He intervenes and delivers miracles. Perhaps the biggest obstacles He can remove are the ones in our own hearts that keep us from receiving and believing in His love.

The enemy will always tempt you to forget God's faithfulness. It's your job to remember. What are some things you can set up to help you repeatedly remember His past faithfulness?

4. Who are we really struggling with, according to Ephesians 6:12?

We have an adversary: the devil. He does not operate alone; he has an army of demons. The Bible testifies to their existence, the evil in the world confirms it, and Church doctrine has consistently affirmed this reality throughout the centuries. We are fools and easy prey if we deny that the devil is real, but we also don't need to become obsessed and see evil lurking in every shadow. C. S. Lewis addresses this in his book *The Screwtape Letters*: "There are two equal and opposite errors into which our race can fall about the devils. One is to disbelieve in their existence. The other is to believe, and to feel an excessive and unhealthy interest in them. They themselves are equally pleased by both errors and hail a materialist or a magician with the same delight."[44]

---

[44] C. S. Lewis, *The Screwtape Letters* (New York: HarperCollins, 1996), ix.

For our purposes, it's worth taking a moment to reflect on our current struggles. Whom are we blaming for them? Whom are we pointing to in our minds as "the enemy"? Remember that our adversary, the "father of lies," loves to blind us to truth. Anytime we are experiencing division in a relationship, we can be certain that the enemy is at work, encouraging all parties to see the worst in the other. Can you try to see things from the other person's perspective? Might it help to acknowledge that you do not have all the facts, that it is at least possible that missing information might lead you to a faulty conclusion? It isn't always the case, but it's worth a little self-check, considering our tendency to make up stories in our heads about what is going on.

Quiet your heart and enjoy His presence. . . . The battle is already won.

"As an artist, God makes use even of the devil." —Saint Augustine

Whenever we turn our focus to the work of the enemy, we run the risk of becoming discouraged by all the chaos, division, and evil he causes. In those moments, we must remember that God is always in control, and far more powerful. In the words of author Paul Thigpen, "God allows evil because He's powerful enough to bring out of even the greatest evil a much greater good."

Nowhere do we see this more clearly than on the cross. The very moment that the enemy believed was his greatest victory was actually his defeat. Satan had entered Judas and encouraged countless people to turn against Jesus. It looked as if everything was going according to plan. Little did Satan know, the very thing he thought would destroy Jesus simply destroyed death. Jesus appeared to be hanging powerless on the cross, but He was actually in the process of freeing us all from slavery to sin.

What appears to be hopeless in your life? Where do you feel like the enemy has the upper hand? Shift your focus from the people and the circumstances onto the artist. God, your loving Father, has the brush in hand, and He is creating a masterpiece with your life and the life of your loved ones. He is at work. God will reshape the very thing the enemy intends to use to take you down into something that brings you growth and blessing. Hold on to that hope.

We are promised in Isaiah 54:17 that no weapon fashioned against us and intended for our destruction shall prevail. What the enemy intends for evil, God will use for good. We feel the stab of the weapon and worry it means our death. God reminds us that after Good Friday, we have Easter. We have the Resurrection. That very thing that seems dead and hopeless? God can breathe new life into it. Hold on to hope.

Day Two
HOLD YOUR GROUND

Read Ephesians 6:13.

1. What instructions are we given in Ephesians 6:13?

What is meant by "hold your ground"? It's staking a claim to your territory and not letting the enemy steal even an inch. It means that when you are under attack, you don't move. It's remaining steadfast even when you are weary, even as you face your greatest fears, even when your wounds feel raw. Has the enemy knocked you down? Holding your ground means that *you get back up*—again and again and again.

There's a little phrase tucked in the middle of this verse that is going to be our focus for this section: *having done everything*. It describes a wholehearted Warrior who keeps searching and stretching until she has every possible weapon tucked into her arsenal.

Some of the best weapons aren't usually seen as such. All too often, they are either ignored or considered spiritual to-dos. Even when we know that these things draw us closer to God, we don't always realize just how much they are strengthening us and forming us into Warriors.

Later in this lesson and then in the final talk we'll look at the weapons and armor of Scripture, prayer, and the sacraments. But if we are going to *have done everything*, then we will also grab hold of these often-overlooked weapons: worship, fasting, and adoration. Let's unpack each one.

2. In his book on spiritual warfare, author Paul Thigpen writes, "Worship is a spiritual weapon. When we worship God, we enter into His presence in a powerful way. Because demons tremble at His presence, they are reluctant to follow us there."[45] Psalm 27:5–6 describes the protection of God's presence. According to these verses, what does the psalmist do when he is in the tent of God?

---

[45] Thigpen, *Manual for Spiritual Warfare*, 39.

When we are going through a time of suffering and difficulty, offering worship is truly a sacrifice. Our instinct is to complain, rage, or curl up in a ball. This is what the enemy expects us to do. But when we go against our instinct and choose to worship instead, it delivers a blow. In worship, we turn our focus to God and away from our circumstances. This loosens the power of the enemy's tactics.

Pastor and founder of the Passion Movement Louie Giglio shares powerfully about a season in his life when he experienced debilitating anxiety and found that worship was the way out for him. He woke in the middle of the night with an intense panic attack, and things began to spiral from there. He took medications to help reset his body, and as he shared with others what he was going through, he found person after person who was experiencing something similar or who knew someone who had. Maybe that's where you are today, or where you've been. If it is, please know you are not alone.

Consistently at two a.m., Louie would feel the cloud, the pit, and the dread coming. One night in particular, he called out to God, telling Him that he could not endure this one more night. It was too awful, too dark, too much. What he wanted more than anything was a quick change, a fast solution. But the anxiety was continuing. The Holy Spirit brought Job 35:10 to mind, reminding him that God "gives songs in the night." Louie responded in prayer by saying, "Lord, if you'll give me a song in the night, I'll sing it to you." The following lyrics came to him:

Be still, there is a healer
His love is deeper than the sea
His mercy, it is unfailing
His arms are a fortress for the weak

Louie stayed on that thought throughout the night until morning. What was happening as he did this? In his own words, "Whenever we feel the cloud or the pit or the dread coming, underneath all of that is the fear and the dread the enemy brings to us. We combat that [through worship] by setting our eyes back on the greatness and grandeur of God."[46] Worship was not a quick fix for Louie, but it was a powerful weapon to fight back the darkness and a critical part of his finding a deeper peace.

Personally, worship music has been my lifeline, the cry of my soul, and my comfort. The playlist for *Fearless and Free* at walkingwithpurpose.com includes the songs that are currently reframing my perspective and reminding my heart and mind of the goodness and tenderness of God. I hope they encourage you, too.

---

[46] Louie Giglio, interviewed by James and Betty Robison, "Life Today," http://www.lightsource.com/ministry/life-today/louie-giglio-a-song-in-the-night-501247-full.html.

3. What do the following verses promise is accomplished when we wield the weapon of fasting?

Isaiah 58:6

Daniel 9:3, 21–23 (Note what Daniel did, and who came as a result of his prayer.)

"If prayer is a spiritual weapon, fasting is the spiritual whetstone[47] on which it is sharpened. It's the spiritual muscle that, when exercised regularly, strengthens the thrust of that weapon to pierce the enemy and drive him away." —Paul Thigpen

We read in CCC 2043 that fasting "helps us acquire mastery over our instincts and freedom of heart." While we want to always avoid excesses and we need to use fasting with discernment, it can be a powerful way for us to be spiritually strengthened. Even with a decision to say no to something small that we want, we are reminded that mastering our instincts does not kill us. We are able to walk away from things that we like and desire. We're reminded that "He who is in you is greater than he who is in the world" (1 John 4:4).

Quiet your heart and enjoy His presence. . . . Wield the weapon of adoration.

Saint John Bosco talked frankly about the devil and the strength gained through praying in front of the Blessed Sacrament. He shared the following in his memoirs:

Listen: There are two things the Devil is deathly afraid of: fervent Communions and frequent visits to the Blessed Sacrament.

Do you want Our Lord to grant you many graces? Visit Him often.
Do you want Him to grant you only a few? Visit Him only seldom.
Do you want the devil to attack you? Rarely visit the Blessed Sacrament.
Do you want the Devil to flee from you? Visit Jesus often.
Do you want to overcome the Devil? Take refuge at Jesus' feet.
Do you want to be overcome by the Devil? Give up visiting Jesus.

---

[47] whetstone: an abrasive stone for sharpening knives or other edged tools

Visiting the Blessed Sacrament is essential if you want to overcome the Devil. Therefore, make frequent visits to Jesus. If you do that, the Devil will never prevail against you.[48]

Notice that he didn't say you wouldn't ever feel the sting of one of the enemy's attacks. But he did promise that the devil would never prevail against you. This means that you can be brave enough for today—brave enough to hold your ground—because Jesus is fighting for you.

Day Three
ARMOR UP

You are a part of a monumental battle, and God does not want you to be caught by surprise or to be unarmed when an attack occurs. Because you have experienced the Wakening, you are less likely to be caught unaware. You know there is a battle and have learned what's at stake. You might wonder if you are unarmed. No, you aren't—not if you've been applying what you've been studying. As we have journeyed through the book of Ephesians, you have actually been handed weapons and armor all along.

But now that we are coming to the close of the study, we're bringing it all together into a visual of how a Warrior suits up for battle. Ephesians 6:14–17 paints a picture of the whole armor of God, available to each one of us, every day. We have a choice—to walk into the day naked or dressed like a fighter. Knowing about our armor and actually putting it on are two different things. As my friend Sister Miriam Heidland says, "Too often we head into the battle wearing a Speedo and carrying a water gun." What a visual. No wonder we feel slaughtered. There are better clothes to wear.

Read Ephesians 6:14–15.

1. A. What should be fastened around your waist? See Ephesians 6:14.

Fastening the belt of truth means that we agree with God about what He says is true. This was a critical part of the Wakening. In Lessons 2-3 (Chosen), we learned the truth about our identity and destiny. Anytime you start to question your worth, go back and review that lesson. In Lesson 4-5 (Grounded), we learned about what truly gives us security and rootedness. We looked at the reality of the battle, and recognized that we've been wounded. This lesson reminded us that those wounds

---

[48] Thigpen, *Manual for Spiritual Warfare*, 40-41.

can be healed, and that God can be trusted with the most tender places of our hearts.

In the battle, the enemy will attack you by *distorting truth*. You need to counter that with a *declaration of truth*. Use the I Declares in Appendix 5 to help you do this. Let this be a springboard to write your own I Declares, based on the unique lies that take you down. Turn to Appendix 5 now, so you know where to go when you need it.

If you need to be reminded of your true identity as a beloved daughter, use Appendix 6 and read "Who I Am in Christ."

If we want to live a life of true, ongoing freedom, we have to regularly saturate ourselves with the truth. Just because we've read it once, or even done this Bible study, doesn't mean we won't need reminding. We will need to saturate our minds with these truths day after day for the rest of our lives. The lies have made sense to us for too long, and deprogramming or reframing our thinking takes time. Keep pulling this Bible study off your shelf to go back and review these lessons. We *all* need to do this in order to continue looking at life through a renewed and cleaned lens.

B. As you reflect on this study and the response you just had as you read "The I Declares" and "Who I Am in Christ," can you identify certain truths that are hard to hold on to? List them here.

Note: The extent to which the truth doesn't seem true indicates that this is an area of struggle. You will want to read daily and even memorize the verses associated with that particular truth. This is how you can "be transformed by the renewing of your mind" (Romans 12:2). If you want help in learning how to do this, see Appendix 7: "Scripture Memory."

2. A. Which piece of armor should we put on next, according to Ephesians 6:14?

A Roman soldier's breastplate covered the most important organ for life: his heart. Worn over a leather garment, the bronze breastplate reached down to the soldier's thighs. In that same way, the breastplate of righteousness protects our hearts. While the belt of truth is about knowing what's right and true, the breastplate of righteousness is about *doing* it.

The enemy of our soul prowls around and looks for a chink in the armor—a spot where he can shoot an arrow. When we do what God has asked us to do, it seals up those chinks and limits the enemy's access to our hearts.

This was a big focus for us in the Wrestling. We were challenged in Lessons 6-7 (Mature) to speak the truth in love, be renewed in the spirit of our minds, and put on the new self. Instead of sitting down halfway up the hill, we decided to get up, get moving, and do what we know to be right and true. In Lessons 8-9 (Passionate), we were challenged to be imitators of God. God is passionate about our holiness. Because of this, He allows us to feel discomfort when our choices are leading us down the wrong path. He wakes us up when we're complacent or flirting with darkness. This doesn't feel good, but it's for our good.

B. As you reflect on your journey in *Fearless and Free*, do you have some unfinished business to take care of? Does your breastplate of righteousness need some polishing? Are there some chinks in the armor? Take a peek at your resolutions from lessons 6 and 8. How are you doing in keeping them? If you are struggling to keep your resolutions (most of us are—you're in good company), write a prayer resolving again to pursue God's best in this area of your life. Failing is a part of progress. The problem comes when we stop getting back up and trying again.

Dear Lord,

I recommit to obeying you in the following area of my life:

3. A. What are we told to put on our feet? See Ephesians 6:15.

The soles of Roman soldiers' shoes were made of leather layers held together with nails. The nails were metal studs that gave them a firm grip in the dirt, the way cleats do. When a soldier dug his feet into the ground as he fought, he was strong and firm. His feet were protected, and He was always ready to move and fight.

We, too, want to be firm-footed. Regardless of what is thrown at us in life, we want to be operating from a place of stability and security. This verse tells us that our ability to be grounded comes from the gospel of peace.

The gospel of peace has been woven throughout this study. I pray you have grasped hold of it and deeply inhaled the unearned favor of God. It's yours because you are His precious daughter. The gospel of Jesus tells us that God's love for us isn't based on our hustle, performance, or perfection. It has nothing to do with what we have done and everything to do with what Jesus already did. *We need to preach the gospel to ourselves every day.* This is how we dig our feet into the ground. Our default is a self-reliant mode of trying to prove our worth. This is the opposite of a posture of dependence that keeps us close to God.

So we preach the gospel to ourselves, and then strap on the shoes of peace so we can carry this message to our loved ones who are completely worn out and longing for something more. Our message of peace says that there is a totally different way to live. There is freedom. It's possible to let go of the "white-knuckle it and try hard" life and rest in God's grace.

B. Take a moment and think about three people you know and love who haven't yet grasped hold of the gospel of grace. Write their names here. Could it be that God wants your feet to travel a little closer to theirs to share the difference He has made in your life? Write out 1 Peter 3:15 below their names.

One way we can be prepared to share the gospel of peace is by watering the ground ahead of time with our prayers. Seeds of faith take root in soil that has been watered by our intercession, sometimes accompanied by tears.

When the ground is fertile, you need to be ready to share the difference Jesus has made in your life. It's not necessary to share everything you know. You don't even need to know very much. One thing I'll bet you *do* know is what your life would be like without Jesus. And I pray you have tasted the difference that He can make. Your before-and-after story should be very simple and short, opening the door to further conversation and questions without sounding spiritually superior, judgmental, or long-winded. Pastor Bill Hybels describes it this way:

It's worth searching your heart and soul to firm up the three-pronged foundation of your story: the key word or concept that describes who you were before you met Christ; the fact that you then came into a relationship with Christ; and the key word or concept that describes who you are after walking with Christ for a time.[49]

Give it a try here:

Before Jesus:

(Some ideas to get you started: I was striving; I was empty; I was gripped by fear; I was self-destructive)

I encountered Christ personally in this way:

(Ideas: a friend invited me to Bible study; a person explained things to me in a way that finally made sense; I attended an event or retreat; I was struggling and experienced Him answering my prayer)

This is the difference He has made:

(Ideas: I've found peace; I feel fulfilled; I have courage; I treat myself kindly; I'm healthy; I'm more balanced)

One of the most compelling ways we can share our faith is to be honest about our times of suffering and struggle. Instead of trying to act like we have it all together, we can be honest about parts of our current life or past that frankly feel like a complete mess. This is disarming and authentic, and if shared in a mature way, it invites or draws people closer. When we then share the difference Jesus has made in those moments of difficulty, people start to get a glimpse of a "faith that works"

---

[49] Bill Hybels, *Just Walk Across the Room* (Grand Rapids, MI: Zondervan Publishing, 2006), 126-127.

in the day-to-day grind. Not that there isn't an appropriate time for sharing the facts, truths, and core teachings about our faith, but I believe our own vulnerable sharing is more likely to open a heart.

Quiet your heart and enjoy His presence. . . . Remember, His heart is tender toward you.

"My soul is downcast within me; therefore I remember you." (Psalm 42:7)

It can be a hard thing, this remembering. I can have a great perspective on life—one full of gratitude and awareness of God's goodness—and then suffering slams into me and I start to reel. I begin to question, and all too often, I allow my thoughts to dwell on the doubts instead of all the times Jesus has come through for me and the difference He has made in my life. I have to discipline myself to strap on the belt of truth and remember:

~The gospel of grace says nothing I do will increase or decrease my worth or acceptance by God.

~I am the beloved daughter of the King.

~Being a beloved daughter of the King gives me authority over the enemy.

~God has a plan for my life.

~His plan is for my good.

~God will not abandon me in this moment.

It takes discipline to stop the spiral of negative thinking and instead dwell on the heart of the Father. It means I have to take my eyes off my circumstances and turn them to what I know to be true. Even if it isn't our natural response to hardship, we can choose this attitude instead. It can be done.

Strap on the belt of truth and read those truths again, but this time, say them out loud. Declare them. Claim the victory that is yours, because as a beloved daughter of the King, you have authority over any spirit of discouragement, hopelessness, and fear. Claim your birthright.

Day Four
RAISE YOUR SWORD

Read Ephesians 6:16–17.

1. A. What does Ephesians 6:16 say we should hold as a shield? What does this shield quench?

B. What do we learn about faith from Hebrews 11:1, 6?

The Roman soldier's shield was a triangular shape, and when he crouched down, it covered his whole body. Made of wood, canvas, leather, and iron, the shield was soaked in water so that it could extinguish the flaming arrows shot by the enemy. This description makes me think of a daughter of God crouched down in prayer. Her faith acts like a force field, shielding her heart from fiery arrows. She rises, fortified, a Warrior of supernatural strength.

Without faith, we can't please God and we lack the strength to fight the spiritual battle. So what do we do when our faith takes a hit? In his work as a licensed psychologist and marriage, family, and child counselor, Dr. James Dobson has witnessed the impact of suffering on people's faith. He has this to say about what causes the most difficulty during crushing circumstances:

> It is an incorrect view of Scripture to say that we will always comprehend what God is doing and how our suffering and disappointment fit into His plan. Sooner or later, most of us will come to a point where it appears that God has lost control—or interest—in the affairs of people. *It is only an illusion*, but one with dangerous implications for spiritual and mental health. Interestingly enough, pain and suffering do not cause the greatest damage. **Confusion is the factor that shreds one's faith** [emphasis added] . . . The human spirit is capable of withstanding enormous discomfort, including the prospect of death, *if the circumstances make sense.*[50]

---

[50] James Dobson, *When God Doesn't Make Sense* (Carol Stream, IL: Tyndale House, 2012), 13.

Here's the problem. All too often, on the surface, suffering does *not* make sense. We wrestle with the question, "If we are following you, God, if we are doing what we are supposed to be doing, why is this so hard?"

I just asked that question recently to my trusty counselor, the all-wise Sarah. She leaned in, eyes and heart full of gentleness, and said, "Our culture equates hard with bad, and easy with good. But what if that's wrong? What if hard is actually good? Sometimes marriage is hard work, but isn't that when something really good is being created? What if we are looking at things from the wrong perspective?"

I've been chewing on that thought as I walk through some pretty intense suffering. I don't *want* hard = good, but I think she's right. Every single hard thing I am experiencing has the potential to bring great good—*if my heart is utterly captured by Jesus*. If I am passionate about knowing, serving, and pleasing Him, then hard circumstances that refine me in those areas are actually good.

My friends and family are strongly discouraging it, but I am so tempted right now to tattoo the word *fiat* on my wrist. Since ink washes off and doesn't cause my mother trauma, I just keep writing the word on my skin. Every time I catch sight of it, I remind myself that I want to be like Mary. What a Warrior. I want to be like her, desiring God's will above all else. And I want to come to a point of maturity where regardless of my circumstances, I am able to say, "This is hard. But this is God's will. So somehow, even though I don't understand, this is *good*."

C. Is confusion because of suffering causing your faith to take a hit? In what area of your life do you believe God is asking you to accept His will, to give your fiat, even when questions remain unanswered?

On those nights when anxiety gets the better of me and I can't sleep, I battle in bed with my rosary in hand. I picture myself lifting up the shield of faith as I launch into the Apostles' Creed. The creed becomes the battle cry of my faith when I inwardly shout, "This is what I believe!" Sometimes I feel the belief; other times I just choose to cling to the creed as truth. I settle underneath that shield, and get to work praying. I dedicate each decade of the Rosary to an overall concern in my heart, and then before each Hail Mary, I ask the Lord for something specific. On especially faith-filled nights, I am able to devote a decade to the things that I am grateful for. This practice has given me a whole new perspective regarding sleeplessness. It takes away some of the confusion and frustration usually associated with it, and infuses those nights with purpose.

2. A. What piece of armor should be covering your head? See Ephesians 6:17.

    B. What do the following verses and Catechism clip say we must do in order to be saved?

    Mark 16:16

    Acts 2:21

    CCC 977

    C. What has the Church provided so that we can receive forgiveness when we fall into sin after having been baptized? See CCC 980.

When we are adopted as beloved daughters of God in baptism, we are accepted and forgiven. This is "our right by grace, the full right of love" (CCC 2009). We can rest in this. Salvation was provided for us by Jesus.

A woman who thinks she has to be perfect to earn God's love has left her helmet of salvation on the table. Her mind is unprotected, and the enemy will fire arrows of doubt about her worthiness all day long.

Salvation is God's free gift to us, something we cannot earn. We strap on the helmet of salvation by remembering this and then staying close to Him. We call on His name, have faith that He is good and will come through for us, and confess whenever we wander.

3. A. So far, all our weapons have been for our defense and protection. Ephesians 6:17 unveils an *offensive* weapon. What is it?

Roman soldiers carried two different swords. One was heavy and required two hands to wield. The other was smaller, about eighteen inches long—more like a dagger. This is the one Paul is talking about in this verse. Both of its edges were sharp, and the point was sharp as a needle. This one was used for hand-to-hand combat; it could be easily hidden and easily reached.

B. Revelation 1:16 describes Jesus as holding seven stars in His right hand, with something coming out of His mouth. What is it?

C. How is the Word of God described in Hebrews 4:12?

The Word of God—the sword of the Spirit—is living and active. It's not static; it's dynamic. It is moving in your life and in my life at the same time but in different ways. It's sharper than any two-edged sword, meaning it can go somewhere with pinpoint accuracy and hit the mark. It goes deep in our hearts and starts to reveal our motives—why we do what we do. It starts to reveal our thoughts. It starts to unearth the hurts that we have buried.

Until we have allowed the sword of the Spirit to have its way within our hearts, we won't be as effective wielding it as an offensive weapon against the enemy. I know that some wounds have likely been unearthed for you during this study. My hope is that as you have moved through the pages of Ephesians, you have encountered the Great Physician, the healer of your soul, in a deeper way. I pray you have given Him access to your brokenness.

This is an ongoing process, like the peeling of an onion. But be assured, each time something is peeled back in our hearts, revealing our need for the healing touch of the Savior, the restoration goes deeper. And God promises us that we will come out on the other side stronger, fortified, and better equipped for battle.

So even if you feel shaky, even if you feel that there is healing work left to be done, I echo the words of author and speaker Lisa Bevere: "Face forward, stand your ground, lift your sword and let the enemy see the lovely face of a hero." [51]

Quiet your heart and enjoy His presence. . . . He makes heroes in the hidden and broken places.

I recently read a quote by poet W. H. Auden: "We would rather be ruined than changed." Our pride, revealed in our desire to be in control and in charge, can really get in the way of experiencing the transformation and freedom that God provides us.

By contrast, the psalmist in Psalm 131 writes, "I do not concern myself with great matters or things too wonderful for me. But I have stilled and quieted my soul; like a weaned child with its mother, like a weaned child is my soul within me." This picture of childlike dependence reminds me of the Warrior who is willing to crouch down under the shield of faith during times of confusion.

It isn't so hard to exercise faith when everything is going our way. But when suffering hits and we don't know why, our natural response is to question God's goodness and perhaps competence, demanding an explanation instead of crouching down in prayer.

In the very moment that you want to question why, I challenge you to hide yourself under the shield of faith and ask God to make you into a hero. In that very moment when you feel most broken and discouraged, ask God to supernaturally infuse you with His divine strength, power, and virtue. The process may feel unbearable, but I promise you, you will not be ruined. God will never give you more than you can bear if you rely on Him. Jesus told us in John 12:24 that "unless a grain of wheat falls to the ground and dies, it remains just a grain of wheat; but if it dies, it produces much fruit." But it doesn't just produce fruit. It produces heroes who stand their ground, raise their swords, and experience victory.

Day Five
OVERCOME AND CONQUER

Read Ephesians 6:18–20.

---

[51] Lisa Bevere, *Girls With Swords: How to Carry Your Cross Like a Hero* (Colorado Springs, CO: WaterBrook Press, 2013), 52.

"Prayer, without a doubt, is the most powerful weapon the Lord gives us to conquer evil . . . but we must really put ourselves into the prayer. It is not enough just to say the words; it must come from the heart. And also prayer needs to be continuous. We must pray no matter what kind of situation we find ourselves in. The warfare in which we are engaged is ongoing, so our prayer must be ongoing as well."
—Saint Alphonsus Liguori

1. Read the following verses and record any insights into what helps us to wield the weapon of prayer more effectively.

2 Chronicles 7:14

Psalm 66:18

1 John 5:14

Presenting our requests to God while praying for His will to be done can be incredibly difficult. When Jesus prayed, "My Father, if it is not possible for this cup to be taken away unless I drink it, may your will be done" (Matthew 26:42), He was sweating blood. If we are praying honestly, embracing God's will usually involves some serious wrestling.

We can just throw out the words "your will be done" as a little cap to our prayers. Or we can do the work of getting to the bottom of why we are leery or afraid of His will. I believe that if we drill down to the heart of it, we are worried that God's will is going to include suffering, and we are desperate to avoid that. We question the heart of the Father, wondering if He is truly good.

Scottish evangelist Oswald Chambers wrote, "We must pray with our eyes on God, not on the difficulty." He is good, He is faithful, He is for us, and He is our protector. He is the restorer of all things broken, including dreams and hearts. So we center our thoughts on who God is, and then pray the words of Mark 9:24: "Lord, I do believe; help me overcome my unbelief!"

2. Author Ann Voskamp gently challenges us, "Be brave and do not pray for the hard thing to go away, but pray for a bravery that's bigger than the hard thing."[52] What hard thing are you facing? Can you write a prayer below, asking God for a bravery that is bigger than the hard thing?

Sometimes when we are suffering, we don't have the words or the energy for verbose prayers. God understands. The simple gesture of an unclasped hand lifted to Him can be worth a thousand words when it represents our heart's surrender.

Saint Teresa of Ávila's wisdom takes the pressure off our shoulders and gives suffering a new perspective: "One must not think that a person who is suffering is not praying. He is offering up his sufferings to God, and many a time he is praying much more truly than one who goes away by himself and meditates his head off, and, if he has squeezed out a few tears, thinks that is prayer." Some of our greatest Warriors are the hidden heroes who suffer greatly while offering it up to the Lord. No tear, no heartache, no pain is wasted when it is accompanied by a surrendered heart.

We lift our hands and claim the promise of Romans 8:26: "The Spirit helps us in our weakness. We do not know what we ought to pray for, but the Spirit himself intercedes for us through wordless groans." And that is more than enough.

3. A. In Daniel 10, the angel Gabriel appeared to the Old Testament prophet Daniel. What did the angel come in response to, and when did he set out? See Daniel 10:12.

   B. If he set out from the first day Daniel started to pray, why didn't the angel Gabriel arrive sooner? Who came to Gabriel's aid so he could continue on to Daniel? See Daniel 10:13.

   This section of Scripture is one of the few that draw the curtain back and give us insight into the spiritual battle that rages in the heavenly realm. We don't see what

---

[52] Ann Voskamp, *The Broken Way* (Grand Rapids, MI: Zondervan, 2016), 167.

is going on all around us, but the battle between good and evil is real. It involves angels and demons.

Incredibly, *our prayers impact this battle.* In his book *Angels and Demons: What Do We Really Know About Them?* author Peter Kreeft writes, "I strongly suspect that if we saw all the difference even the tiniest of our prayers to God make, and all the people those little prayers were destined to affect, and all the consequences of those effects down through the centuries, we would be so paralyzed with awe at the power of prayer that we would be unable to get up off our knees for the rest of our lives."[53]

C. What three specific things did Daniel do that caused the angel Gabriel to come to his aid? See Daniel 10:12.

"Since that first day that you _____ to . . .

Acquire _____ and _____

before your God, your prayer was heard. Because of it I started out."

This is what we have been endeavoring to do throughout the journey of *Fearless and Free.* We have made up our minds to stop letting thoughts and fears run through our heads freely. Determining to take every thought captive to Christ, we are following the steps Saint Ignatius laid out for us—to **be aware** that not all the thoughts in our mind come from God, to **understand** if the thought is a truth or a lie, and to **take action**, rejecting the lie and embracing the truth.

Our growth in self-awareness has hopefully made us more humble. We know we have wounds and struggles with sin. Instead of numbing our hearts or blaming others, we are seeking healing and wholeness. We recognize this is a journey. In 1 Peter 5:6 we are told to "Humble yourselves, therefore, under God's mighty hand, that he may lift you up in due time."

Warrior, He is lifting you up. It is time for you to arise. You are not alone. You are "surrounded by such a great cloud of witnesses, [so] let us throw off everything that hinders and the sin that so easily entangles. And let us run with perseverance the race marked out for us!" (Hebrews 12:1).

---

[53] Peter Kreeft, *Angels and Demons: What Do We Really Know About Them?* (San Francisco, CA: Ignatius Press, 1995), 205.

Quiet your heart and enjoy His presence. . . . The battle is won or lost on our knees.

"Prayers outlive the lives of those who uttered them; outlive a generation, outlive an age, outlive a world." —E. M. Bounds

Your prayers move mountains, call down angels, and turn the battle. Their impact can go beyond your lifetime. Prayer is the secret of the fiercest Warrior—her source of strength, understanding, peace, and victory.

The following psalms are powerful prayers; God loves to hear His own words confidently prayed back to Him.

"Lord, for you alone my soul waits in silence, for my hope is in you. You alone are my rock and my salvation, my fortress; because of you, I shall not be shaken. My deliverance and my honor rests on you; my mighty rock, my refuge. I will trust in you at all times. I pour out my heart before you because you are my refuge." (Psalm 62:5–8)

"I am seeking you God, knowing that you will answer me and deliver me from all my fears. I am looking to you, and pray that you would make my face radiant. Remove all shame from me. I have cried out to you and you have heard me and saved me out of all my troubles. Thank you for sending the angel of the Lord to encamp around me and deliver me." (Psalm 34:4–7)

One last verse, because it is so true and we need this reminder every day:

"But the Lord stood with me and he strengthened me." (2 Timothy 4:17)

You are never, ever alone. God sees you; He hears you; He is with you.

Conclusion

I wish I could promise that if you follow all the principles we've learned in Ephesians, the battle will be clean, predictable, and not too bloody, but I cannot.

The truth is, the enemy of your soul fights dirty. He strikes where you feel weakest. Oftentimes, your hardest battles will be hidden ones. The loneliness this causes might feel unbearable. The relentlessness of his attacks will take you by surprise. The perseverance required will sometimes leave you weary.

Many of us who remain on the battlefield in spite of this—those who refuse to give up—are harboring the question, "Why? Why does it have to be so brutal? Why is there so little letup? Why does one more thing slam into me just when I've said I can't take any more?" As we dwell on these questions, sometimes afraid to say them out loud, our shoulders droop and our heads fall to our chests.

And Jesus comes. He cups our face in His hands, lifting our gaze to His. "Look at me," He says.

"Who is your commander?" He asks.

And perhaps most important, "*Where* is your commander?"

He rises up strong, and shares with us the vision of Revelation 19:11–13, 16:

> Then I saw the heavens opened, and there was a white horse; its rider was called "Faithful and True." He judges and wages war in righteousness. His eyes were like a fiery flame, and on his head were many diadems. He had a name inscribed that no one knows except himself. He wore a cloak that had been dipped in blood, and his name was called the Word of God. . . . He has a name written on his cloak and on his thigh, "King of kings and Lord of lords."

This is our commander. He rushes to our side with eyes flaming with passion. Our rescuer rages against the evil that has hurt us. He has not left us to fight the battle alone. When it wages the fiercest, He draws the closest. When we can't bear another minute, He hides us and gives us rest. He doesn't answer the question of why, but *He comes for us*, Faithful and true. Our King of kings and Lord of lords fights for us and never leaves our side.

> He who dwells in the shelter of the Most High,
> who abides in the shadow of the Almighty
> will say to the LORD, "My refuge and my fortress; my God, in whom I trust."
> For He will deliver you from the snare of the fowler and from the deadly pestilence;
> He will cover you with His pinions, and under His wings you will find refuge;
> His faithfulness is a shield and buckler.
> You will not fear the terror of the night,
> Not the arrow that flies by day,
> Nor the pestilence that stalks in darkness,
> Nor the destruction that wastes at noonday.

A thousand may fall at your side,
Ten thousand at your right hand;
But it will not come near you.
You will only look with your eyes
And see the recompense of the wicked.
Because you have made the LORD your refuge,
The Most High your habitation,
No evil shall befall you,
No scourge come near your tent.

For He will give His angels charge of you,
To guard you in all your ways.
On their hands they will bear you up,
Lest you dash your foot against a stone.
You will tread on the lion and the adder,
The young lion and the serpent you will trample underfoot.

Because he clings to Me in love, I will deliver him;
I will protect him, because he knows My name.
When he calls to Me, I will answer him;
I will be with him in trouble,
I will rescue him and honor him.
With long life I will satisfy him,
And show him my salvation. (Psalm 91:1–16)

Our commander is the game changer.

What a Savior. What a lover of our souls. What a rescuer.

Never lose hope. With Jesus, you always belong. With Jesus, you are faithfully loved. With Jesus, there is no shame. With Jesus, love chases away fear. With Jesus, the path ahead is cleared. With Jesus, you have an unlimited source of power at your disposal. With Jesus, you are never alone.

"The Lord, your God, is in your midst, a warrior who gives victory; He will rejoice over you with gladness, He will renew you in His love." (Zephaniah 3:17)

My Resolution

In what specific way will I apply what I have learned in this lesson?

Examples:

1. I will start each day by praying Ephesians 6:14–19 over my life:

    Dear God,
    Help me to stand firm today. Please fasten the belt of truth around my waist and protect my heart with the breastplate of righteousness. May my feet be fitted with the shoes of peace so I am ready to share the gospel. May I take up the shield of faith and use it to extinguish the flaming arrows of the evil one. Place the helmet of salvation over my head—my mind—and help me to remember that I am safe and secure in you. May I wield the sword of the Spirit (the Word of God) in such a way that I rebuke lies and embrace truth. Amen.

2. I want to strengthen the thrust of the weapon of prayer in my life. In order to do this, I commit to fasting for a specific prayer intention.

3. I have identified certain truths, listed in the appendices "The I Declares" and "Who I Am in Christ," that are hard for me to believe. I will memorize a Bible verse this week that corresponds to one of those truths so that the Holy Spirit can bring it to my mind when I need reminding.

My resolution:

Catechism Clips

CCC 409   This dramatic situation of "the whole world [which] is in the power of the evil one" makes man's life a battle:

> The whole of man's history has been the story of dour combat with the powers of evil, stretching, so our Lord tells us, from the very dawn of history until the last day. Finding himself in the midst of the battlefield man has to struggle to do what is right, and it is at great cost to himself, and aided by God's grace, that he succeeds in achieving his own inner integrity.

CCC 977 Our Lord tied the forgiveness of sins to faith and Baptism: "Go into all the world and preach the gospel to the whole creation. He who believes and is baptized will be saved." Baptism is the first and chief sacrament of forgiveness of sins because it unites us with Christ, who died for our sins and rose for our justification, so that "we too might walk in newness of life."

CCC 980 It is through the sacrament of Penance that the baptized can be reconciled with God and with the Church:

> Penance has rightly been called by the holy Fathers "a laborious kind of baptism." This sacrament of Penance is necessary for salvation for those who have fallen after Baptism, just as Baptism is necessary for salvation for those who have not yet been reborn.

CCC 2015 The way of perfection passes by way of the Cross. There is no holiness without renunciation and spiritual battle. Spiritual progress entails the ascesis and mortification that gradually lead to living in the peace and joy of the Beatitudes:

> He who climbs never stops going from beginning to beginning, through beginnings that have no end. He never stops desiring what he already knows.

NOTES

Looking for more material? We've got you covered! Walking with Purpose meets women where they are in their spiritual journey. From our Opening Your Heart 22-lesson foundational Bible study to more advanced studies, we have something to help each and every woman grow closer to Christ. Find out more:

www.walkingwithpurpose.com

Lesson 11

BRAVE TALK

Accompanying talk can be viewed by DVD or digital download purchase or access online at walkingwithpurpose.com/videos.

I. The Infusing Power of the Sacraments

"Sacraments are like hoses. They are the channels of the living water of God's grace. Our faith is like opening the faucet. We can open it a lot, a little, or not at all."[54] –Peter Kreeft

The belt of truth is fortified by _____.

Colossians 1:13

Galatians 3:27

When we are WRESTLING and stepping out as WARRIORS, we need to grab hold of the weapon of PRAYER. There's no prayer more powerful than the

_____.

"In the EUCHARIST, Christ has given to those who desire Him the ability not only to see Him, but even to touch Him, eat Him, fix their teeth in His flesh, and embrace Him, to satisfy all their love. For this reason, we must return from that Table like lions breathing fire, having become terrifying to the Devil. We must be thinking about Christ our head, and about the love He's shown to us."
–Saint John Chrysostom

---

[54] Peter Kreeft, *Jesus Shock* (FL: Beacon Publishing 2008), 117.

When we are in the thick of the battle, we've also got to be sure to strap on the BREASTPLATE OF RIGHTEOUSNESS. Nothing keeps that breastplate in better condition than the sacrament of _____.

The SWORD OF THE SPIRIT can be wielded in _____, not to cause harm or win an argument, but to speak God's words of truth and hope directly into the heart of a spouse with laser-like precision.

CONFIRMATION is another sacrament that strengthens us as WARRIORS. To confirm means "_____." Saint Thomas Aquinas described Confirmation as the sacrament where spiritual strength is conferred, making the recipient a _____ for the faith of Christ.

II. The Victory in Simply Not Quitting

John 12:24

Discussion Questions

1. After hearing the ways in which the sacraments strengthen us for battle, do you have an increased desire to receive any of them with greater openness and frequency? If so, which one(s), and why?

2. Which of your weapons or spiritual armor has been sitting on your shelf? What are you going to do in order to step into the battle dressed and armed for victory?

3. As you look back on your journey through Fearless and Free, what spiritual and emotional growth do you see?

Appendices

NOTES

Appendix 1
SAINT THÉRÈSE OF LISIEUX

Patron Saint of Walking with Purpose

Saint Thérèse of Lisieux was gifted with the ability to take the riches of our Catholic faith and explain them in a way that a child could imitate. The wisdom she gleaned from Scripture ignited a love in her heart for her Lord that was personal and transforming. The simplicity of the faith that she laid out in her writings is so completely Catholic that Pope Pius XII said, "She rediscovered the Gospel itself, the very heart of the Gospel."

Walking with Purpose is intended to be a means by which women can honestly share their spiritual struggles and embark on a journey that is refreshing to the soul. It was never intended to facilitate the deepest of intellectual study of Scripture. Instead, the focus has been to help women know Christ: to know His heart, to know His tenderness, to know His mercy, and to know His love. Our logo is a little flower, and that has meaning. When a woman begins to open her heart to God, it's like the opening of a little flower. It can easily be bruised or crushed, and it must be treated with the greatest of care. Our desire is to speak to women's hearts no matter where they are in life, baggage and all, and gently introduce truths that can change their lives.

Saint Thérèse of Lisieux, the little flower, called her doctrine "the little way of spiritual childhood," and it is based on complete and unshakable confidence in God's love for us. She was not introducing new truths. She spent countless hours reading Scripture and she shared what she found, emphasizing the importance of truths that had already been divinely revealed. We can learn so much from her:

> The good God would not inspire unattainable desires; I can, then, in spite of my littleness, aspire to sanctity. For me to become greater is impossible; I must put up with myself just as I am with all my imperfections. But I wish to find the way to go to Heaven by a very straight, short, completely new little way. We are in a century of inventions: now one does not even have to take the trouble to climb the steps of a stairway; in the homes of the rich, an elevator replaces them nicely. I, too, would like to find an elevator to lift me up to Jesus, for I am too little to climb the rough stairway of perfection. So I have looked in the

books of the saints for a sign of the elevator I long for, and I have read these words proceeding from the mouth of eternal Wisdom: "He that is a little one, let him turn to me" (Proverbs 9:16). So I came, knowing that I had found what I was seeking, and wanting to know, O my God, what You would do with the little one who would answer Your call, and this is what I found:

"As one whom the mother caresses, so will I comfort you. You shall be carried at the breasts and upon the knees they shall caress you" (Isaiah 66:12–13). Never have more tender words come to make my soul rejoice. The elevator which must raise me to the heavens is Your arms, O Jesus! For that I do not need to grow; on the contrary, I must necessarily remain small, become smaller and smaller. O my God, You have surpassed what I expected, and I want to sing Your mercies. (Saint Thérèse of the Infant Jesus, *Histoire d'une Ame: Manuscrits Autobiographiques* [Paris: Éditions du Seuil, 1998], 244.)

Appendix 2
NOTHING BUT THE BLOOD OF JESUS

What's up with all the talk about blood? It can really offend our modern sensibilities, seeming barbaric and even a little creepy.

We have to look back to the Old Testament to understand where it is coming from. The Jewish people had always been taught that life was "in the blood," and that there was sacredness to it. We can understand this today, recognizing that blood supplies our body with all the nutrients it needs, then carries waste away from our cells. Without blood, we couldn't survive.

Blood was integral to worship for the Jewish people. Through it, they were reconciled to God and cleansed of sin. Let me explain how this worked.

God commanded the Israelites to make daily sacrifices of animals to atone for their sins. Atonement was the process of making amends for sin. It was the way they compensated for wrongdoing. Another word for atonement is *satisfaction*. When the sacrifice was offered, God was satisfied and forgave.

How did this work? The Israelite people would bring an unblemished animal to the courtyard outside the temple and place their hands on it, and their sin would be transferred to the innocent animal. The animal was slaughtered on the altar in their place. In exchange for the life of the animal, God offered forgiveness. This may seem to us like a strange way to deal with sin, but in Leviticus 17:11, God had said that the life of an animal was found in its blood. So its life—its blood—was to be used "to make atonement [amends] on the altar . . . it is the blood . . . that makes atonement." We see this again in Hebrews 9:22: "According to the law almost everything is purified by blood, and without the shedding of blood there is no forgiveness."

Within the temple was an inner room, the Holy of Holies, which was separated from the rest of the temple by a veil. This was no see-through veil that a bride might wear. The Mishnah (the recorded oral tradition of Jewish law) says that the veil was the thickness of a man's hand—around six inches. It was enormous. It's said that it was sixty feet high—almost six stories—and twenty feet wide. It took three hundred priests to hoist it and move it into place. It was imposing and delivered a strong message: DO NOT ENTER.

Why was this place so protected? The Holy of Holies was the place where God dwelled. This was a sacred place, because it was there that God had promised to meet with man.

Only one person was allowed to enter the Holy of Holies: the high priest. And he wasn't allowed whenever he wanted. He was permitted to enter once a year, on Yom Kippur, the Day of Atonement. On this day, he came in with blood from sacrificed animals, and asked forgiveness for the sins of all the people. This is described in Hebrews 9:6: "The priests, in performing their service, go into the outer tabernacle [or Holy Place] repeatedly, but the high priest alone goes into the inner one once a year, not without blood that he offers for himself and for the sins of the people."

While the temple sacrifices provided a means for the Israelites to be forgiven for their sins, it also delivered the steady message: *You are not holy. God is. You have no right to stand in His presence.*

Keeping this reality in mind, fast-forward to Jesus hanging on the cross. In Matthew 27:50–51, we read that at the end of His earthly life, Jesus "cried out again in a loud voice, and gave up his spirit. And behold, the veil of the sanctuary was torn in two from top to bottom. The earth quaked, rocks were split." God tore the veil right down the middle. This isn't something that a man could have done. Remember, it was six inches thick and sixty feet high. It was said that even horses tethered to its corners couldn't rip it apart.

Can you imagine the chaos that resulted from this gaping tear? For hundreds of years, hardly anyone had seen behind this curtain—only the high priest, once a year. And suddenly, everyone could look inside. The torn veil symbolized a monumental change in the way God was to relate to man. Everything had changed.

What did the high priest have to carry in order to enter into God's presence in the Holy of Holies? He had to enter with blood, year after year. And no one else was allowed in.

But now, as it says in Hebrews 10:19–20, "through the blood of Jesus, we have confidence of entrance into the sanctuary by the new and living way he opened for us through the veil . . ."

The priests in the Old Testament had to offer the same sacrifices over and over again. Day after day, innocent animals were killed in place of people to atone for their sin. But these sacrifices never dealt permanently with the problem of sin. As we are told in Hebrews 10:1–9, the old plan was only a hint of the good things in the new plan. Since that old "law plan" wasn't complete in itself, it couldn't complete those who followed it. No matter how many sacrifices were offered year after year, they never added up to a complete solution. If they had, the worshippers would have gone merrily on their way, no longer dragged down by their sins. But instead of removing awareness of sin, when those animal sacrifices were repeated over and over, they actually heightened awareness and guilt. The plain fact is that bull and goat blood can't get rid of sin.

The final substitution for sin—the final atonement, the final innocent substitute for man—had to be offered to God the Father in heaven. What was happening on earth was a copy, a shadow. An innocent substitute—a perfect atonement—would need to be presented in heaven in order for sin to be permanently dealt with.

The book of Hebrews describes this in chapter 9:23-24: "Therefore, it was necessary for the copies of the heavenly things to be purified by these rites [the sprinkling of blood], but the heavenly things themselves by better sacrifices than these. For Christ did not enter into a sanctuary made by hands, a copy of the true one, but heaven itself, that he might now appear before God on our behalf."

Jesus' blood was put on the heavenly mercy seat. Hebrews 9:12 says, "He entered once for all into the sanctuary, not with the blood of goats and calves but with his own blood, thus obtaining eternal redemption."

Jesus entered the sanctuary with His own blood, and appeared before God on our behalf. He entered on behalf of all the people who had lived throughout the Old Testament, who looked forward to a redemption yet to come. He entered on behalf of the people who lived when He walked the earth—the very ones who had called out for His crucifixion. He entered on behalf of all those who would be born after the time of His incarnation. We are in that group. He appeared before the Father as the ultimate atonement. Remember that atonement is the process of making amends for sin. It's the way of compensating for wrongdoing. Another word for *atonement* is *satisfaction*. **When God the Father looked on the blood of His perfect Son, Jesus, He was satisfied.** He was satisfied with that sacrifice, and offered forgiveness for anyone covered with Jesus' blood.

Jesus is able to be the perfect sacrifice because he is both God and man. As St. Anselm says, "It was fitting that a man atone for the sins of men, but only God could atone for the kind of offense that sin is. Jesus Christ is both God and man, and thus the perfect sacrifice." (See also CCC 615-616).

Do you want access to the Father? Do you want to enter the Holy of Holies and come into His presence? Do you long to be ushered into His heart?

You need to enter His presence with blood, but not the blood of animals. You need to enter with the blood of Jesus.

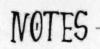 NOTES

Appendix 3
CONVERSION OF HEART

The Catholic faith is full of beautiful traditions, rituals, and sacraments. As powerful as they are, it is possible for them to become mere habits in our lives, instead of experiences that draw us close to the heart of Christ. In the words of John Paul II, they can become acts of "hollow ritualism." We might receive our first Communion and the sacraments of confession and confirmation, yet never experience the interior conversion that opens the heart to a personal relationship with God.

Pope Benedict XVI has explained that the "door of faith" is opened at one's baptism, but we are called to open it again, walk through it, and rediscover and renew our relationship with Christ and His Church.

So how do we do this? How do we walk through that door of faith so we can begin to experience the abundant life that God has planned for us?

Getting Personal

The word *conversion* means "the act of turning." This means that conversion involves a turning away from one thing and a turning toward another. When you haven't experienced conversion of heart, you are turned *toward* your own desires. You are the one in charge, and you do what you feel is right and best at any given moment. You may choose to do things that are very good for other people, but the distinction is that *you are choosing*. You are deciding. You are the one in control.

Imagine driving a car. You are sitting in the driver's seat, and your hands are on the steering wheel. You've welcomed Jesus into the passenger's seat, and have listened to His comments. But whether you follow His directions is really up to you. You may follow them or you may not, depending on what seems right to you.

When you experience interior conversion, you decide to turn, to get out of the driver's seat, move into the passenger's seat, and invite God to be the driver. Instead of seeing Him as an advice giver or someone nice to have around for the holidays, you give Him control of every aspect of your life.

More than likely, you don't find this easy to do. This is because of the universal struggle with pride. We want to be the ones in charge. We don't like to be in desperate need. We like to be the captains of our ships, charting our own courses. As William Ernest Henley wrote, "I am the master of my fate: I am the captain of my soul."

Conversion of heart isn't possible without humility. The first step is to recognize your desperate need of a savior. Romans 6:23 states that the "wages of sin is death." When you hear this, you might be tempted to justify your behavior, or compare yourself with others. You might think to yourself, "I'm not a murderer. I'm not as bad as this or that person. If someone were to put my good deeds and bad deeds on a scale, my good ones would outweigh the bad. So surely I am good enough? Surely I don't deserve death!" When this is your line of thought, you are missing a very important truth: Just one mortal sin is enough to separate you from a holy God. Just one mortal sin is enough for you to deserve death.[55] Even your best efforts to do good fall short of what God has required in order for you to spend eternity with Him. Isaiah 64:6 says, "All our righteous acts are like filthy rags." If you come to God thinking that you are going to be accepted by Him based on your "good conduct," He will point out that your righteousness is nothing compared to His infinite holiness.

Saint Thérèse of Lisieux understood this well, and wrote, "In the evening of my life I shall appear before You with empty hands, for I do not ask You to count my works. All our justices are stained in Your eyes. I want therefore to clothe myself in Your own justice and receive from Your love the eternal possession of Yourself."[56]

She recognized that her works, her best efforts, wouldn't be enough to earn salvation. Salvation cannot be earned. It's a free gift. Saint Thérèse accepted this gift, and said that if her justices or righteous deeds were stained, then she wanted to clothe herself in Christ's own justice. We see this described in 2 Corinthians 5:21: "God made him who had no sin to be sin for us, so that in him we might become the righteousness of God."

How did God make Him who had no sin to be sin for you? This was foretold by the prophet Isaiah: "But he was pierced for our transgressions, he was crushed for our iniquities; the punishment that brought us peace was upon him, and by his wounds we are healed" (Isaiah 53:5).

Jesus accomplished this on the cross. Every sin committed, past, present, and future, was placed on Him. Now *all the merits of Jesus can be yours*. He wants to fill your empty hands with His own virtues.

But first, you need to recognize, just as Saint Thérèse did, that you are little. You are weak. You fail. You need forgiveness. You need a savior.

---

[55] "One sin was enough to merit death for the first human beings who were in the state of preternatural perfection. For us, joined to Christ in His Body, one mortal sin merits death. Venial sin does not, although venial sin makes it easier to commit mortal sin. See CCC #1854-#1864."

[56] Saint Thérèse of Lisieux, "Act of Oblation to Merciful Love," June 9, 1895.

When you come before God in prayer and acknowledge these truths, God looks at your heart. He sees your desire to trust Him, to please Him, to obey Him. He says to you, "My precious child, you don't have to pay for your sins. My Son, Jesus, has already done that for you. He suffered so that you wouldn't have to. I want to experience a relationship of intimacy with you. I forgive you.[57] Jesus came to set you free.[58] When you open your heart to me, you become a new creation![59] The old you has gone. The new you is here. If you will stay close to me, and journey by my side, you will begin to experience a transformation that brings joy and freedom.[60] I've been waiting to pour my gifts into your soul. Beloved daughter of mine, remain confident in me. I am your loving Father. Crawl into my lap. Trust me. Love me. I will take care of everything."

This is conversion of heart. This act of faith lifts the veil from your eyes and launches you into the richest and most satisfying life. You don't have to be sitting in church to do this. Don't let a minute pass before opening your heart to God and inviting Him to come dwell within you. Let Him sit in the driver's seat. Give Him the keys to your heart. Your life will never be the same again.

---

[57] "If we acknowledge our sins, he is faithful and just and will forgive our sins and cleanse us from every wrongdoing." (1 John 1:9)

[58] "So if the Son makes you free, you will be free indeed." (John 8:36)

[59] "So whoever is in Christ is a new creation: the old things have passed away; behold, new things have come." (2 Corinthians 5:18)

[60] "I will sprinkle clean water over you to make you clean; from all your impurities and from all your idols I will cleanse you. I will give you a new heart, and a new spirit I will put within you. I will remove the heart of stone from your flesh and give you a heart of flesh." (Ezekiel 36:25–26)

NOTES

Appendix 4
WHEN IT'S DIFFICULT TO FORGIVE

Forgiving those who have hurt us is really hard and sometimes beyond what we can do without divine intervention. The following prayer by Francis MacNutt, taken from his book *The Practice of Healing Prayer*, can help release your heart so you can freely forgive.

Lord Jesus Christ,

Send your Holy Spirit into my life and fill me with your love for people. Especially in regard to _____ [name], whom I have a hard time forgiving, help me to see him [or her] as you see him. Take out of my heart the desire to get even. Show me some good quality in him that I haven't seen before. I pray that you bless this person in abundance. Free me from any judgmentalism on my part, and help me to love the person as you do. If he needs to change, help him do that, but help me to change too, and show me any areas where I may be blind. Pour out your love into my heart. Forgive me my sins as I forgive those who have hurt me.

Give me the power through your Spirit for my hidden self to grow strong, so that Christ may live in my heart through faith. And then, planted in love and built on love, I will have strength to grasp the breadth and the length, the height and the depth until, knowing the love of Christ, I am filled with the utter fullness of God. (The last part of this prayer is based on Ephesians 3:16–19.)[61]

---

[61] Francis MacNutt, *The Practice of Healing Prayer* (Frederick, MD: The Word Among Us, 2010), 97.

NOTES

Appendix 5
THE I DECLARES

THE I DECLARES

~ I declare that I am a beloved daughter of the King.

~ I declare that being a beloved daughter of the King gives me authority over the enemy.

~ I declare that God has a plan for my life.

~ I declare that His plan is for my good.

~ I declare that God will not abandon me in this moment.

🌿 FEAR OF THE FUTURE

Counter your what-ifs with the truth.

~ I declare that God has not given me a spirit of fear, but a spirit of power, love, and a sound mind (2 Timothy 1:7).

~ I declare that you are my peace, not perfect circumstances (Ephesians 2:14).

~ I declare if I present my requests to you with a spirit of gratitude, your peace will guard my heart and mind (Philippians 4:6–7).

~ I declare that if I seek first your kingdom and righteousness, then all the things I need will be given to me as well (Luke 12:31).

~ I declare that if I trust in you with all my heart and don't lean on my own understanding, you will make my path straight (Proverbs 3:5–6).

~ I declare that God's plans for me are to prosper me and not harm me, to give me a hope and a future (Jeremiah 29:11).

PAIN FROM THE PAST 🌿

Counter your if-onlys with the truth.

~ I declare God has thrown my sin as far as the east is from the west (Psalm 103:12).

~ I declare God will restore the years the locusts have eaten (Joel 2:25).

~ I declare that if I confess my sin, God is faithful and just and will forgive it (1 John 1:9).

~ I declare that when you forgive, my sins that were like scarlet become as white as snow (Isaiah 1:18).

~ I declare that you are doing a new thing in my life: You are making a way in the wilderness and streams in the wasteland (Isaiah 43:19).

~ I declare that I am a new creation in Christ. The old is gone. The new is come (2 Corinthians 5:17).

🌿 CURRENT SUFFERING

Counter the discouragement and hopelessness with the truth.

~ I declare that when I am weak, you are strong within me (2 Corinthians 12:10).

~ I declare that no temptation has seized me except that which is common to man. And you will always provide a way out so that I can stand up under it (1 Corinthians 10:13).

~ I declare that God will restore, support, strengthen, and establish me (1 Peter 5:10).

~ I declare that no amount of suffering can separate me from the love of God (Romans 8:35).

~ I declare that I am uniquely equipped to provide comfort to others because I truly understand. The comfort you've given me can be poured out to others who are suffering in the same way I am (2 Corinthians 1:3–4).

~ I declare that my light and momentary troubles are achieving for me an eternal glory that far outweighs them all (2 Corinthians 4:17).

STRUGGLE IN MARRIAGE

Counter the heaviness with the truth.

~ I declare God's arm is not too short to save us. He can reach into my heart
and into my husband's heart and draw the two of us together (Isaiah 59:1).

~ I declare that if you are for us, who can be against us (Romans 8:31).

~ I declare that I can hold firmly to hope, because you, the One who
promised, are faithful (Hebrews 10:23).

~ I declare that when we lack love, you can give us divine love for each other (Romans 5:5).

~ I declare that what God has joined together, no one should separate (Mark 10:9).

~ I declare that you are our lamp, and you can turn our darkness into light (2 Samuel 22:29).

WORRY ABOUT YOUR CHILDREN

Counter the feelings of powerlessness with the truth.

~ I declare that you who began a good work in my child will bring it to completion (Philippians 1:6).

~ I declare that you can reach down from on high and take hold of my child,
drawing him out of deep waters (2 Samuel 22:17).

~ I declare that my work as a mother will be rewarded and that my child will come back
from the land of the enemy (Jeremiah 31:16).

~ I declare that there is hope in my future and in my child's future, and that my child
will come back to her own border (Jeremiah 31:17).

~ I declare that all your promises are yes in Jesus, and that not one word of your
promises has ever failed (2 Corinthians 1:20; 1 Kings 8:56).

~ I declare that you are able to accomplish abundantly more than all
I could ask or imagine (Ephesians 3:20).

DOUBTING THE GOODNESS OF GOD

Counter the loss of trust with the truth.

~ I declare that just because I don't understand what you are allowing does not mean
you are not good. I declare that your thoughts are not my thoughts, and your ways
are not my ways. For as the heavens are higher than the earth, so are your ways higher
than my ways, and your thoughts than my thoughts (Isaiah 55:8–9).

~ I declare that your grace and goodness sometimes visit in uncomfortable forms. "You wound and you
heal" (Deuteronomy 32:39). But you allow the wound so that we heal more deeply.

~ I declare that you are gracious, slow to anger, and abounding in steadfast love and faithfulness, keeping
steadfast love for the thousandth generation, forgiving iniquity, transgression, and sin (Exodus 34:6–7).

~ I declare that you are a sun and shield, that you give grace and glory. I declare that you don't withhold
any good thing from those who walk uprightly (Psalm 84:11).

~ I declare that your steadfast love never ceases; your mercies never come to an end. They are new
every morning. I declare that great is your faithfulness (Lamentations 3:22–23).

~ I declare that you are good—a stronghold in the day of trouble. I declare that you know
those who take refuge in you (Nahum 1:7).

STRUGGLE WITH BEING SINGLE

Counter the discontentment with the truth.

~ I declare that I do not need to be afraid, that I will not be put to shame. I do not need to fear disgrace because I will not be humiliated. (Isaiah 54:4)

~ I declare that my Maker is my husband- the Lord Almighty is His name. The Holy One of Israel is my Redeemer. (Isaiah 54:5)

~ I declare that you will have compassion on me with everlasting kindness. (Isaiah 54:8)

~ I declare that there is a time for everything, and a season for every activity under the heavens. (Ecclesiastes 3:1)

~ I declare that if I seek first your kingdom and your righteousness, all these things will be given to me as well. (Matthew 6:33)

~ I declare that I do not need to worry about tomorrow. (Matthew 6:34)

~ I declare that if I trust in you with all my heart and don't lean on my own understanding, you will make my path straight. (Proverbs 3:5-6)

~ I declare that charm is deceptive and beauty is fleeting, but a woman who fears the Lord is to be praised. (Proverbs 31:30)

~ I declare that you heal the brokenhearted and bind up my wounds. (Psalm 147:3)

~ I declare that I can be strong and courageous because you go with me and will never leave me or forsake me. (Deuteronomy 31:6)

~ I declare that God sets the lonely in families. (Psalm 68:6)

~ I declare that if I take delight in you, Lord, if I experience joy in your presence, you will give me the desires of my heart. (Psalm 37:4)

~ I declare that you will never let me be tempted beyond what I can bear. When I am tempted, you will always provide a way out so that I can endure it. (1 Corinthians 10:13)

~ I declare that in Christ, I have been brought to fullness. I am complete in Christ. (Colossians 2:10)

~ I declare that now is not a time for me to wallow in pity. I declare that I am God's handiwork, created in Christ Jesus to do good works, which you prepared in advance for me to do. (Ephesians 2:10)

~ I declare that when I'm unmarried, I can live a life of undivided devotion to you. But a married woman is also concerned about how she can please her husband. (1 Corinthians 7:34-35)

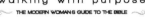

walking with purpose
THE MODERN WOMAN'S GUIDE TO THE BIBLE

# NOTES

Appendix 6
WHO I AM IN CHRIST

Do you wonder who you are? Do you struggle to define your worth by the right things? Read the following verses and rest in the truth that you are God's beloved daughter. You are worthy. You are accepted. You are loved.

I Am God's Beloved Daughter and That Is Enough

"In love, [God] destined us for adoption to himself through Jesus Christ" (Ephesians 1:4–5).
I am not an orphan. I am God's beloved daughter.

"The one begotten by God he protects, and the evil one cannot touch him" (1 John 5:18b).
I am God's daughter. He protects me. The evil one cannot touch me.

"For in [Jesus] dwells the whole fullness of the deity bodily, and you share in this fullness in him, who is the head of every principality and power" (Colossians 2:9–10).
I am complete in Christ.

I Am a New Creation

"So whoever is in Christ is a new creation: the old things have passed away; behold, new things have come" (2 Corinthians 5:17).
I am a new creature in Christ.

"No longer I, but Christ lives in me; insofar as I now live in the flesh, I live by faith in the Son of God who has loved me and given himself up for me" (Galatians 2:20).
Christ lives in me.

"Put on the new self, which is being renewed, for knowledge, in the image of its creator" (Colossians 3:10).
I am done with my old life. My new self is being made in the image of my Creator.

I Am Forgiven

"In him we have redemption by his blood, the forgiveness of transgressions, in accord with the riches of his grace that he lavished upon us" (Ephesians 1:7–8).
I am forgiven for all my sins.

"He himself bore our sins in his body upon the cross, so that, free from sin, we might live for righteousness. By his wounds you have been healed" (1 Peter 2:24).
I am healed by Christ's wounds.

"If we acknowledge our sins, he is faithful and just and will forgive our sins and cleanse us from every wrongdoing" (1 John 1:9).
When I confess my sins, God forgives me, every time.

I Am Free and Fully Alive

"But God, who is rich in mercy, because of the great love he had for us, even when we were dead in our transgressions, brought us to life with Christ (by grace you have been saved)" (Ephesians 2:4–5).
I am alive with Christ, saved by grace.

"For the law of the spirit of life in Christ Jesus has freed you from the law of sin and death" (Romans 8:2).
I am free from the law of sin and death.

I Am Strong and Courageous

"In justice shall you be established, far from oppression, you shall not fear, from destruction, it cannot come near" (Isaiah 54:14).
I am free from oppression, and fear will not master me.

"The one who is in you is greater than the one who is in the world" (1 John 4:4).
The One in me is greater than the evil one.

"For God did not give us a spirit of cowardice but rather of power and love and self-control" (2 Timothy 1:7).
God has not given me a spirit of fear, but one of power, love, and a sound mind.

"In all circumstances, hold faith as a shield, to quench all the flaming arrows of the evil one" (Ephesians 6:16).
I can quench all the fiery darts of the evil one with my shield of faith.

"I can do all things through Christ who strengthens me" (Philippians 4:13).
I can do all things through Christ.

"In all these things we conquer overwhelmingly through him who loved us" (Romans 8:37).
I am more than a conqueror through Him who loves me.

"They conquered him by the blood of the Lamb and by the word of their testimony; love for life did not deter them from death" (Revelation 12:11).
I am an overcomer by the blood of the Lamb and the word of my testimony.

I Am Filled With God's Peace

"We have the mind of Christ" (1 Corinthians 2:16).
"Have among yourselves the same attitude that is also yours in Christ Jesus" (Philippians 2:5).
I have the mind of Christ.

"Then the peace of God that surpasses all understanding will guard your hearts and minds in Christ Jesus" (Philippians 4:7).
I have the peace of God that surpasses all understanding.

 NOTES

Appendix 7
SCRIPTURE MEMORY

"The tempter approached and said to him, 'If you are the Son of God, command that these stones become loaves of bread.' He said in reply, 'It is written: One does not live by bread alone, but by every word that comes forth from the mouth of God" (Matthew 4:3–4).

Jesus was able to respond to Satan's temptations because He knew God's truth. When He was under fire, He didn't have time to go find wisdom for the moment. It had to already be in His head. He had memorized Scripture, and found those words to be His most effective weapon in warding off temptation.

Do you ever feel tempted to just give in? To take the easy way when you know the hard way is right? Does discouragement ever nip at your heels and take you to a place of darkness? If you memorize Scripture, the Holy Spirit will be able to bring God's truth to your mind just when you need to fight back.

Ephesians 6:17 describes Scripture as an offensive weapon ("the sword of the Spirit"). How does this work? When negative thoughts and lies run through our minds, we can take a Bible verse and use it as a weapon to kick out the lie and embrace the truth. Verses that speak of God's unconditional love and forgiveness and our new identity in Christ are especially powerful for this kind of battle. When we feel defeated and like we'll never change, when we falsely assume that God must be ready to give up on us, the Holy Spirit can remind us of 2 Corinthians 5:17: "If anyone is in Christ, [she] is a new creation. The old has gone. The new has come!"

That's not the only way memorized Scripture helps us. The Holy Spirit can bring one of the truths of the Bible to our mind just before we might make a wrong choice. It's like a little whisper reminding us of what we know is true, but there's power in it, because we know they are God's words. For example, in the midst of a conversation in which we aren't listening well, the Holy Spirit can bring to mind Proverbs 18:2: "Fools take no delight in understanding, but only in displaying what they think." This enables us to make a course correction immediately instead of looking back later with regret. As it says in Psalm 119:11, "I have hidden your word in my heart *that I might not sin against you*" (emphasis added).

You may think of memorizing Scripture as an activity for the über-religious, not for the average Christian. A blogger at She Reads Truth (shereadstruth.com) describes it this way: "Recalling Scripture isn't for the overachievers; it's for the homesick." It's for those of us who know that earth isn't our home—heaven is. It's for those of us who don't want to be tossed all over the place by our emotions and instead long to be grounded in truth.

But how do we do it? Kids memorize things so easily, but our brains are full of so many other bits of information that we wonder if we're capable of doing it. Never fear. There are easy techniques that can help us to store away God's words in our minds and hearts. Pick a few that work for you! *You can do it!*

1. Learning Through Repetition

Every time you sit down to do your Bible study, begin by reading the memory verse for *Fearless and Free, which is Ephesians 3:20*. The more you read it, the sooner it will be lodged in your memory. Be sure to read the reference as well. Don't skip that part—it comes in handy when you want to know where to find the verse in the Bible.

2. Learning Visually

Write the memory verse *in pencil* on a piece of paper. Read the entire verse, including the reference. Choose one word and erase it well. Reread the entire verse, including the reference. Choose another word and erase it well. Reread the entire verse, including the reference. Repeat this process until the whole verse has been erased and you are reciting it from memory.

3. Learning Electronically

Go to our website under Courses and save the *Fearless and Free* Memory Verse Image to your phone's lock screen. Practice the verse every time you grab your phone.

4. Learning by Writing It Down

Grab a piece of paper and write your verse down twenty times.

5. Learning by Seeing It Everywhere

Display the gorgeous WWP memory verse card somewhere in your house. Recite the verse each time you pass by it. But don't stop there: Write your verse down on index cards and leave them in places you often linger—the bathroom mirror, the car dashboard, whatever works for you.

6. Learning Together

If you are doing this Walking with Purpose study in a small group, hold each other accountable and recite the memory verse together at the start and end of each lesson. If you are doing this study on your own, consider asking someone to hold you accountable by listening to you say your verse from memory each week.

Now to Him who is able to do IMMEASURABLY MORE THAN ALL WE ASK OR IMAGINE, ACCORDING to his power THAT IS AT WORK within us.

EPHESIANS 3:20

walking with purpose

NOTES

Appendix 8
SMALL GROUP LEADER'S GUIDE

With a heart full of gratitude, I want to thank you for your willingness to step out and lead women toward a closer relationship with Christ through *Fearless and Free*! Without your dedication, many women's good intentions would remain just that. But your willingness to serve as a leader means women will have the opportunity to take the next step—moving beyond talking about the change they'd like to see to actually experiencing transformation.

This study travels deep within the heart. As I wrote, I refused to just settle for intellectual gains when I knew that what Jesus most wants to do is meet each of us in the "holy of holies" in our souls, bringing healing to the places we often hide.

This means that your primary job as a leader is to create a safe space for women to explore and journey. You do not need to have all the answers. In fact, you will be most effective as a leader when you simply accompany the women, acknowledging that you, too, need healing and wholeness.

Even if you have done a lot of soul work, the truth is, spiritual maturity is like the peeling of an onion. It isn't done in an instant, and we often re-visit areas of hurt even years after we thought we were "finished." This isn't because the healing wasn't real. It's because God is taking us to a deeper place.

The truth is, healing is messy. It can't be scheduled, there aren't short cuts, and the release of honest emotions is a big part of it. For it to be genuine, it must be real. Often, we prefer buttoned up and filtered, but in the long run, that leads to bondage. So thank you for holding "sacred space" for your tribe of women. I am praying for you on the journey, and am a fellow pilgrim.

This guide offers you tips and suggestions, but the most important thing is to let the Holy Spirit be your guide. Trust Him when He prompts you to pause and lean in. Skip the questions that feel perfunctory and prioritize discussion that uncovers what's been buried. Therein lies the fruit and the healing that will last.

May the Holy Spirit open over us and pour out courage and freedom.

Roadmap of *Fearless and Free*

Things will never change.
I'm all alone.
I am unlovable.
I am out of control.
It's all up to me.

Have any of these thoughts ever run through your mind? Did you know that each of them is based on a lie?

The tricky thing about lies is that we rarely hear them. They influence our sense of worth and our ability to hope, but they've swirled around us for so long that they've become like background noise. It's time for us to identify the lies that are robbing us of the life of freedom that we were created for and replace them with God's truth.

I promise you—there is more. Are you ready to taste it?

We *can* experience freedom and wholeness on this side of heaven. Healing is not only possible, it is within reach. Developing emotionally healthy habits is attainable. We can grasp hold of joy and live the abundant life Jesus promised in John 10:10.

This is what we are after as we journey through *Fearless and Free*. Along the way, I will be sharing my story with you. My prayer is that it will help you identify the lies that are derailing you. I am honest about my brokenness, and pray it gives you permission to explore yours.

Here's a summary of where we're going…

Introduction

Lesson 1: *Freedom Talk* gives an overview of *Fearless and Free*. We'll be introduced to the three parts of our journey: the Wakening, the Wrestling and the Warrior.

The Wakening (Ephesians 1-3)

Lessons 2-3: *Chosen* wake us up to the reality of who we are in Christ. We are chosen, beloved and destined. But our true identity has been stolen and we've been offered a counterfeit in exchange. This occurred in moments when we were wounded. If we want to walk in freedom, we need to identify our wounds and the identity lies we've accepted. Some women will be able to do this right away. For others, it might take the full length of the study to come to terms with their wounds and brokenness.

Lessons 3-4: Grounded point out some of the detours we have taken on the journey. We've gotten off course, and have been wandering in circles, wondering why nothing makes sense. In these lessons, we'll wake up to what will truly give us security and rootedness. We'll recognize how critical it is that we ground ourselves in reality, grace, and forgiveness. Hopefully, the women will begin to identify specific times of suffering when they have agreed with lies. Following the trail of hurt is key, and the purpose is not to blame others or dwell on the negative. It's to expose lie-based thinking that stands in the way of freedom.

The Wrestling (Ephesians 4-5)

Lessons 6-7: Mature launch us into spiritual boot camp. These meaty lessons explore what it means to be a mature daughter of God. Part of this process is determining to be a victim no longer. Instead, we'll learn to recognize our triggers and stop feeling sideswiped. We'll explore the judgments we've made and the ways they have led to harmful beliefs and vows. A key moment of discovery might occur on Lesson 6, Day 2, question 4. Lean in here. Throughout the rest of Lessons 6-7 we'll learn to wrestle with strongholds and wield the Sword of the Spirit (Scripture).

Lessons 8-9: Passionate reveal the ways we wrestle with our desires, the darkness, and relationships. Teachings from St. Ignatius regarding discernment of spirits offer faithful guidance throughout. We'll learn how to take every thought captive to Christ (instead of being tossed around by our emotions), and how to look at suffering from an eternal perspective. All these things are tied together on Lesson 8, Day 3, question 2. When light bulbs start going off here, the women will be well on their way to freedom. Some wounds will surface as family relationships are explored on Lesson 8, Days 4 and 5. The talk in Lesson 9 will reveal the *value* of those wounds and the gift of being stripped down.

The Warrior (Ephesians 6)

Lessons 10-11: Brave equip us to reclaim ground and move forward. We'll continue to explore St. Ignatius' discernment of spirits, recognizing the enemy's tactics and the ways that God is at work. We'll learn more about our weapons and the armor that

God has provided for us. We'll go back through the study and review the tools we've been given so that we don't forget to use them. We'll be equipped, not just to walk in freedom, but to step out and lead our loved ones to healing and wholeness as well.

General Guidelines

1. Plan to meet together for 1 1/2 hours. This allows time for socializing and Bible study lesson discussion, or video viewing and follow up discussion.

2. Prepare your lesson ahead of time. Don't try to wing it– the more familiar you are with the material, the better you'll be able to focus on the women in the group. Step 1 of preparing is to complete the lesson, focusing on your own spiritual growth. Step 2 is to review this Leader's Guide, then highlight the questions/passages that we say you should focus on. You might also want to write out the segue sentences we provide in a different color ink. (You will be reading the tips in the Leader's Guide but writing things down in the corresponding lesson).

3. *Hospitality:* Beauty breaks down barriers, and making an effort to create a welcoming environment goes a long way. Coffee, snacks, flowers…they aren't critical, but if you take the time to create beauty, women will feel pampered and loved. Allow for time at the beginning of your sessions for women to grab coffee and chat. As they build relationships with one another, the barriers will continue to come down and sharing will be enhanced.

4. If you are unable to set aside the full 1 ½ hours to go through the lessons, you will possibly run out of time and be unable to discuss every question. I will let you know which questions are most important in this Leader's Guide. But remember, these are my suggestions. You know the women in your group better than I do. If you know that other questions are more important for where they are at, that's where you should spend your time.

5. Trust the material. Even when you are unable to discuss every question, remember that the deepest work happens when women open up their hearts to the Holy Spirit and the Bible while delving into the study at home. The discussion time will afford new insights but the value of communion with the Lord that will go on privately cannot be underestimated. This, of course, depends on the women actually doing the homework. So encourage them to complete their lessons. It'll make all the difference in terms of what they get out of *Fearless and Free*. If your women consistently don't do their homework, there is no doubt that they will get

less out of the study. But that's between them and the Lord. Rest assured that women will glean something from the discussion even if their preparation was lacking. We're promised in Isaiah 55:11 that God's word never returns void—it always achieves His purpose.

6. As much as possible, you want to keep a conversational tone, rather than question/answer feel. You can do this by paraphrasing questions when appropriate.

7. Remember that you are facilitating discussion, not teaching a class. The majority of the talking should be done by the women in your group.

8. Ask the Holy Spirit to help you to differentiate between a woman delving deeper and a woman going off on a tangent. Other group members will get frustrated if a woman is allowed to hijack the conversation in other directions. Keep the focus on the material in the study. There is plenty there to discuss.

9. Suggestions for timing are included in this guide. Many leaders find it helpful to mark the time in the margins to help track the time. Getting through the lesson in a timely fashion isn't easy. You might consider asking another group member to help you with the timing. This allows you to keep eye contact with the people sharing, trusting that she'll let you know if you need to move along more quickly.

10. This guide introduces a small group technique which allows all of the women to share on more personal questions with a partner, instead of with the whole group. When you bring the women back together after this time of sharing, you might benefit from some transitional sentences in the event that the women don't want to stop their discussion. Here are some suggestions:

"Okay ladies, I know you have more to discuss but I need to keep us on track. Can we come back together now, please?"

"Let's circle back to the group and keep moving through the lesson."

"I'm so glad everyone got a chance to discuss that question. Let's open discussion to the whole group and move on to question_."

FREEDOM TALK

Lesson 1

1. Social time: **10 minutes**

2. Welcome the women in your small group: **5 minutes**

3. Watch the video (stream it or use a DVD): **30 minutes**

   Point out the outline available in the book and encourage note taking during the video.

4. Small Group Discussion: **45 minutes**

   - *Small Group Welcome (5 min)*
     Begin by introducing yourself and warmly communicating to everyone that, as a small group leader, you are a supporter and friend, not a superior or teacher. WWP is a safe, trusting, friendly environment in which we grow closer to Christ. Explain that you are committed to lead by example by sharing honestly and authentically with them.

   - *Introductions (5 min)*
     In order to get to know one another, you might want to share church affiliation, family, work or what you all hope to gain from *Fearless and Free*. You should go first and then encourage participants to share. Give out index cards, and ask each woman to indicate her preferred contact method: call, text or email.

   - *Introduce the Structure of the Study (5 min)*
     Have the women turn to the Study Guide Format and Reference Materials in the front matter of *Fearless and Free*. This gives a great summary of the study, including the format for study the appendices, supplemental materials, and answer key.

   - *Explanation of Small Group Honor Code (3 min)*
     Read through the Honor Code with your group. The Honor Code can be found at the end of this Leader's Guide section and is also available for download/print on the Walking with Purpose website. Assure participants that they can count on you to follow these guidelines.

- *Share your Commitment as a Small Group Leader (2 min)*
Start on time, and end on time.
No one will be "called on" to answer questions.
Every effort will be made to get through the entire lesson each week, although we may not discuss every question.
Women are welcome to come and discuss even if their lesson isn't finished.

- *Discussion Time (15 minutes)*
Small group leaders lead the Discussion Questions from the talk. These can be found after the outline of the talk in Lesson 1 of *Fearless and Free.*

As you progress through the questions, you may need to share your own answers. But only do this after you have waited for someone else to speak up. If a woman does share, thank her with a warm comment and smile; this will help more hesitant women realize that sharing is enriching and does not have to be intimidating.

- *Prayer Intention Time (10 minutes)*
Have the ladies turn to the back of the study guide to the prayer pages.
The purpose of the prayer intention time is twofold:

1. Explain that part of the small group experience is praying specifically for one another. Each woman is encouraged to write down each woman's name and intention as she is sharing. The whole group is encouraged to offer the intentions to God throughout the week. Prayer intentions are treated with respect and confidentiality. The time is not intended for delving into details that may lead to gossip. When sharing an intention about a struggle with another person, all efforts should be made to keep it general and anonymous.

2. Explain how part of experiencing Christ in a personal way is asking Him for help with our specific needs, and being open to seeing how He transforms, answers and blesses us. While we often think first of the needs of the world and people we care about, WWP encourages the use of this time to specifically ask for prayers for ourselves. For example, you may ask for prayers for patience, for a relationship that needs mending, for the grace to forgive a family member, for family stability, for the grace to manage time better, for peace and freedom from crazy stress, etc. As you move through the study, you'll find that a great way to find a personal prayer request is to turn your "resolution" into a prayer. You can lead by example and remind

women that God is so loving He wants us to ask Him for all of the desires of our heart. We don't need to be afraid to asking for the grace we need, personally.

- *Close in prayer*

CHOSEN BIBLE STUDY

Lesson 2

1. Social time: **10 minutes**

2. Small Group Opening Prayer: The Armor of God/Introduction: **10 minutes**

   Read the Armor of God prayer out loud together, located in the Prayer Pages section. This is a good way to start the small group time and get women settled.

   After praying together, ask, "Did anything in the introduction speak to you personally?" or "What jumped out at you from the introduction?"

3. Day One (Belonging): **10 minutes**

   Summarize **1A** by saying, "St. Paul begins in Ephesians by telling us he was an apostle of Jesus Christ and he held that position by the will of God. We read about the reasons why he wouldn't have been a good choice as a Christian leader, but he somehow was able to see himself as God saw him instead of allowing his past sins to define him."

   Then ask **1B** and allow time for discussion.

   Summarize **2A** by saying, "Ephesians 1:2 greets us with a prayer that we'd have grace and peace. Both are offered to us lavishly, but we have to choose to receive it and empty our hands of our achievements and self-justifications in order to accept them. What did this lesson say we need to experience first—grace or peace?" The answer is grace. We have a choice: to live a life of proving and hustling, or to live a life receiving the free gift of grace—we can't have it both ways.

   Then ask **2B** and allow time for discussion.

   Ask question **3** and allow a quick answer. Ask someone to read the paragraphs following question **3** out loud.

   Ask if anyone wants to share an insight they gained from the *Quiet Your Heart* section. Mention that these parts of the lessons are meant to lead into a time of prayer.

4. Day Two (Adoption): **10 minutes**

Explain that the group will discuss some questions with a partner (instead of with the whole group) to allow for more sharing. We'll use that technique for this question **2**. The women should answer the question with a partner and discuss the commentary that follows. Use the transition sentences provided under **General Guidelines** to bring the group back together.

5. Day Three (Lavish Grace): **10 minutes**

Read question **1,** "In the original Greek, Ephesians 1:3-14 was actually one long sentence…as if one amazing blessing after another was parading in front of St. Paul's eyes. What blessings did he list in Ephesians 1:7-9?" Allow the women to answer. (2 minutes)

Skip to question **3** and have the women turn to their partners to discuss. (5 minutes)

Bring the group back together and read or summarize the commentary following question **3**. (2 minutes)

Skip to question **5** and have the women answer as a group. Ask someone to read the paragraph following it or summarize it in your own words. (1 minute)

6. Day Four (Destiny): **10 minutes**

Read and discuss question **1A** and **1B.** (2 minute)

Skip to question **2** and allow time for discussion. Summarize the commentary below, perhaps sharing the parts you underlined and found interesting. (4 minutes).

Ask question **3,** allow discussion. (2 minutes)
Skip commentary.

Ask question **4A** and **4B**. (2 minutes)

7. Day Five (Enlightenment): **10 minutes**

Summarize question **1** by saying, "Verse 17 tells us why Paul has been teaching us these truths. He's been praying that we'd be given a spirit of wisdom and revelation so that we could know God better. That's the goal. *Not* that we'd become smarter sinners. Paul wants us to know three things. The first is found in question **2A**. What is it?" Answer: the hope that belongs to God's call.

Have the women turn to their partners and discuss the confident expectation we should have, exemplified by the story of the two women in the miserable situation at work. Have them answer question **2B** together as well.

Segue to question **4** by saying, "Paul wanted us to know 3 things- the first was the hope that belongs to God's call. What's the next thing he wants us to know?" Answer: the riches of His glorious inheritance. Note that this isn't talking about the inheritance we'll receive, it's pointing out that God considers *us* His inheritance.

Move to question **4**. Have the women answer **4A** with the whole group, then discuss **4C** with their partners.

8. Conclusion/Resolution: **5 minutes**

Read the Saint John Paul II quote at the start of the conclusion and paraphrase the rest. Point out the importance of making a concrete resolution if we truly want to be transformed. Suggest turning the resolution into the prayer request for prayer intention time.

9. Prayer Intention Time: **15 minutes**

CHOSEN TALK

Lesson 3

1. Social time: **10 minutes**

2. Welcome the women in your small group: **5 minutes**

3. Watch the video (stream it or use a DVD): **30 minutes**

   Point out the outline available in the book and encourage note taking during the video.

4. Small Group Discussion: **30 minutes**

   Discussion questions for the talk are found at the end of the outline in Lesson 3.

5. Prayer Intention Time: **15 minutes**

GROUNDED BIBLE STUDY

Lesson 4

Introduction

1. Social time: **10 minutes**

2. Opening Prayer: The Armor of God/Introduction: **10 minutes**

   After praying together, begin by saying, "This is where we are headed with this lesson… we want to become women who are grounded in reality, grace, belonging, hope and love. To become that kind of woman is going to require not just looking at the things that have shaped us, but also at the sin in our hearts. But before we dive into the lesson, did anything in the introduction speak to you personally?"

3. Day One (Grounded in Reality): **10 minutes**

   Begin by saying, "The truths of Ephesians 2:1-3 aren't intended to lead us to shame. But we need to look at the way sin impacts our lives. I'm hoping that we will be convicted as needed, but never feel shame from what we read. Shame– the sense that I *am* my sin– is different than guilt, which is feeling badly about my sin."

   Summarize question **1** by saying, "Ephesians 2:1 says that when we are apart from Christ, we are dead in our sins and transgressions."

   Move to question **2A**, ask the question, and allow discussion.

   Then say, "Looking at **2B**, how is the ruler of the power of the air, the devil, described?" Allow the women to answer.

   Summarize **2C** by saying, "The third force at work is the 'desires of our flesh'. When we read that list, recognize that we have an enemy working against us, and live in a culture that encourages us to live differently than the way that God desires, it's no surprise why it's so hard to stay on the right track. Would anyone like to share any thoughts from the commentary after question 2?" Allow time for discussion.

Have the women discuss **3A** with a partner.

Bring the group back together and skip to **4Bi,** "What has made us holy and without blemish?"

Then ask **4Bii,** "What did baptism not get rid of within us?"

End by saying, "So clearly, it's going to be a struggle to do the right thing. What do we need? We need to be grounded in grace." Segue to Day Two.

4. Day Two (Grounded in Grace): **10 minutes**

Begin by saying, "After the heaviness of Day 1, our reading for Day 2 starts immediately with the encouraging words of Ephesians 2:4: *But God.*"

As we saw in Day 1, we were dead in our transgressions, but when God intervened, what happened? Let's look at **1B** and **1C**." Allow discussion.

Then say, "After reading the commentary following question **1**, what are your thoughts on why we might have experienced baptism, yet still not feel like God's beloved daughters?"

Ask question **2A**, "How are we saved?" Allow for this short answer, then say, "A critical part of the Wakening is realizing what saves us. It isn't our good works. It isn't our perfection. It isn't the hustle. It's grace at work in our souls."

Ask question **2B**. Allow someone to answer.

Skip to the commentary after question **3**. Say, "Skipping to the commentary after question **3**, we're asked how we are to respond to this unearned gift of grace. Did anyone highlight anything in this section or have something they'd like to share?" Allow discussion.

Move on to question **4**. Ask "How are we described in Ephesians 2:10, and is this how you see yourself?" Allow discussion.

5. Day Three (Grounded in Belonging): **10 minutes**

Intro Day 3 by saying, "This next passage (Eph. 2:11-22) is talking about the alienation and separation that existed between the Jewish people and the Gentiles before Christ came. The Gentiles were without hope, separated and excluded before Jesus changed everything. We're going to discuss this day's questions with our partners. Pay special attention to question **2**, 'Have you ever felt like an outsider?'" Allow discussion.

Bring the group back together and say, "No matter what experiences have been shared here, I hope you all got the important message from this Day's lesson that regardless of how much you might feel like you don't, you belong. No matter who has rejected you or walked away from you, you belong to God."

6. Day Four (Grounded in Hope): **10 minutes**

Intro Day 4 by saying, "In the reading for Day 4, Paul goes off on a tangent to comfort his readers because he knows that they are struggling with the fact that he is in prison. We can imagine that the people in his life felt that his suffering made no sense, and suffering that seems senseless is the hardest to bear. So Paul set out to lift their perspective higher so they wouldn't lose hope. He wants them to focus in on the mystery that had been revealed to him. Let's look at question **1C**. What is the mystery that was revealed to Paul?" Let people answer.

Have someone read the commentary after **1C**.

Go through **2, 3A** and **3B** quickly.

Have the women turn to their partners to discuss the commentary that follows **3B**.

Bring the women back together and turn to the *Quiet Your Heart*. Ask the women what they thought of the story of pastor Josef Tson.

7. Day Five (Grounded in Love): **10 minutes**

Begin with question **1C** by saying, Ephesians 3:14-17 describes our core—"the most important place in each one of us–our hearts. How is the heart described in CCC 2563?" Let the women answer.

Have the women turn to their partners to share their answer for question **2**.

Conclude Day 5 by moving to the commentary after question **4**. Share this sentence, "Logic and analysis can only take us so far. There comes a point when we simply need the Holy Spirit to go to the depths of our inner self and do the healing work." Share that this is what you hope will happen during the course of the study.

8. Conclusion/Resolution: **5 minutes**

Read this part of the Conclusion, "God has promised us that if we delight ourselves in Him, He'll give us the desires of our hearts (Psalm 37:4). The problem is, we tend to pursue that in the wrong order– we start by running after our desires, and then wind up frustrated when they don't deliver what we are searching for. And this is where Jesus comes in. No matter what we face, He is on our side, offering us comfort and direction every step of the way."

Point out the importance of making a concrete resolution if we truly want to be transformed. Suggest turning the resolution into the prayer request for prayer intention time.

9. Prayer Intention Time: **15 minutes**

GROUNDED TALK

Lesson 5

1. Social time: **10 minutes**

2. Welcome the women in your small group: **5 minutes**

3. Watch the video (stream it or use a DVD): **30 minutes**

   Point out the outline available in the book and encourage note taking during the video.

4. Small Group Discussion: **30 minutes**

   Discussion questions for the talk are found at the end of the outline in Lesson 5.

5. Prayer Intention Time**: 15 minutes**

MATURE BIBLE STUDY

Lesson 6

1. Social time: **10 minutes**

2. Opening Prayer: The Armor of God/Introduction: **10 minutes**

   After praying together, begin by saying, "Lesson 4 moves us into the second phase of our *Fearless and Free* journey, The Wrestling. Let's start our discussion with the end goal in mind. We find it in the *Quiet your Heart* on Day 4. 'If you move in the direction of truth and honesty, this is what your life will look like: you will not need to hide, you will seek out other honest people whom you can trust with your brokenness, you will know that brokenness is a permanent part of the human condition…you will be gracious toward other broken people instead of critical and self-righteous…you will live in constant gratitude for a God who accepts you, brokenness and all.' This is what we are after— that kind of life."

3. Day One (Victims No Longer): **10 minutes**

   Ask question **1A.** Let the women answer.

   Have the women turn to their partners to discuss **1B** and the commentary after it.

   Note: The *Quiet Your Heart* of Day One gave women the opportunity/permission to asking God, "Where were you when I was hurting?" This may have been a moment of healing as women realized that God was always there, and never abandoned them.

4. Day Two (Truth and Love): **15 minutes**

   Begin discussion by saying, "This passage reminds us that growing in maturity is a process. Conversion does not equal maturity; it marks the starting point."

   Then ask question **1A**, and have someone read the commentary after it.
   Ask question **2** and then have the women discuss the commentary after question **2** with their partners.

   Bring the women back together and summarize **3A** by saying, "Matthew 7:1-2 says that we are not to judge others— that the way we judge others will be measured out to us. Discuss **3B** with your partner. Are there any judgments you are holding against someone due to a past or a current experience of hurt?"

Bring the women back together and ask for a volunteer to read the commentary after **3B**.

Have the women discuss any vows they have made with their partner (question **4**).

Bring the women back together. This is a very important moment in the women's journey. Lean in here and make sure questions **3** and **4** made sense. Conclude this day by reading or paraphrasing the commentary after question **4**.

5. Day Three (A Renewed Mind): **10 minutes**

   Have the group quickly answer questions **1** and **2.**

   Skip to the commentary after question **3.** Have someone in the group read it.

   Ask question **4**. Move quickly through the answers.

   Point out that we aren't born knowing how to wield the weapons God has provided for us. Let them know that the talk following this lesson will delve into this further.

6. Day Four (The New Self): **10 minutes**

   Ask question **1A**, then skip to the paragraph before question **2** which begins, "If we refuse to speak truth to one another, instead saying the things that don't matter or talking behind people's backs, we won't see where we need to grow…."

   Ask question **2A** and **B** and move quickly through the answers.

   Have the women turn to their partners to discuss the commentary about righteous and unrighteous anger, paying special attention to **2C**, "Is there a relationship in your life in which you are struggling with anger?"

7. Day Five (Get Moving Up the Hill): **5 minutes**

   Ask question **1A.** Skip to the commentary at the end of question **1**. Ask "What is the opposite of grieving the Holy Spirit?" Have someone in the group read the entire commentary after question **1.**

Segue to the second part of question **2** by saying, "Often times our specific sins aren't what's listed in the Mass reading or in our Bible study reading. We read in question **2** that if we're really going to be serious about rooting out the sin in our lives, we're going to take some additional steps. What do you think about the steps Lisa described, beginning with 'I beg the Holy Spirit to convict me of my secret sins...'?"

Then move on to **2C**, asking if anyone has a person in her life who is able to give honest feedback about areas where they need to grow. And most importantly, ask, "Are you willing to ask him or her for that feedback?"

8. Conclusion/Resolution: **5 minutes**

Read the end of paragraph 4, "We are promised in 1 Timothy 1:7...and commit to climbing the hill to maturity together."

 Point out the importance of making a concrete resolution if we truly want to be transformed. Suggest turning the resolution into the prayer request for prayer intention time.

9. Prayer Intention Time: **15 minutes**

Note: By this point, many women will have begun to recognize and wrestle with their own brokenness. As I said at the start of this guide, some of the women will be quicker to see themselves in the journey. For others, layers of self-protection take time to peel away. Your availability to help them process the questions following the talk will be especially valuable now. If you observe that a group member is starting to come to terms with her wounds/beliefs/vows and isn't sure what to do with it all, it could make a big difference if you met her one-on-one for coffee to allow her to share her story privately. You don't need to have any answers or offer guidance. It's simply offering the gift of "holding space" for her as she processes what is going on in her heart.

MATURE TALK

Lesson 7

1. Social time: **10 minutes**

2. Welcome the women in your small group: **5 minutes**

3. Watch the video (stream it or use a DVD): **30 minutes**

   Point out the outline available in the book and encourage note taking during the video.

4. Small Group Discussion: **30 minutes**

   Discussion questions for the talk are found at the end of the outline in Lesson 7.

5. Prayer Intention Time: **15 minutes**

PASSIONATE BIBLE STUDY

Lesson 8

1. Social time: **10 minutes**

2. Opening Prayer: The Armor of God/Introduction: **10 minutes**

   After praying together, ask, "Did anything in the introduction speak to you personally?" or "What jumped out at you from the introduction?"

3. Day One (Desire): **10 minutes**

   Ask questions **1A** and **B**, and questions **2A** and **B**.

   Conclude this day's discussion by saying, "Day One sheds light on an area of our life that, for many women, holds a lot of regret or pain. We are not going to discuss these questions in the group, not because they are unimportant, but because they are highly personal. If this was an especially thought provoking section of study for you, I encourage you to meet with a counselor or priest to discuss it further."

4. Day Two (Light): **10 minutes**

   Read question **1A** and have a woman answer.

   This next section is a lot of commentary, and the teaching is very important. Read this together as a group, changing a reader with each paragraph.

   Have the women answer question **1B**.

   Skip the rest and move on to Day Three.

5. Day Three (Opportunity): **10 minutes**

   Ask question **1A** and **B**.

   Move to question **2,** emphasizing the fact that the opportunities that we are being given to build the spiritual muscles of self-discipline, trust and faith are the circumstances in our lives that we most want to change or get rid of. Ask the women to discuss question **2** with their partners.

This question can bring women to a real ah-ha moment. If discussion seems rich, use the entire 10 minutes for the women to talk with their partners. If discussion seems staid, bring the group back together and summarize the commentary just before question **4**. Then discuss question **4**.

6. Day Four (Mutual Submission): **10 minutes**

Read the introductory paragraphs of Day 4.

Ask question **1**.

Have a group member read the commentary following it.

Ask question **2** and paraphrase the summary after it.

Ask question **3,** and as soon as a woman gives the answer, say, "The truth is, many of us don't feel like we have been loved in this way. I do not want to negate the importance of acknowledging that pain, but what I really want us to focus on is what *we* can do. So rather than having discussion about the ways in which we have not been loved this way, what are some ideas you got from this lesson about the way in which *you* can love more effectively?"

7. Day Five (Roots): **10 minutes**

Say, "This day's lesson takes a look at the impact of family of origin. It's been said that pain that is not transformed is transmitted to others. I'd like us to take this time to discuss the lesson with our partners, keeping in mind what we learned in **1A,** that we are told in Ephesians 6:1-2 that we are to obey our parents as children, and then honor them when we are older. Taking an honest look at your past is not dishonoring your parents, no matter what you may have been told. You can honor them and still tell the truth. I'd like you to focus on **1C** and **D** and the last part of question **2**."

Bring the group back together and move to the commentary after question **2**. Read or paraphrase it. End your time together by having 3 different group members look up Psalm 68:6, Romans 8:35-39, and Philippians 4:19. Have them read it out to the group in order to end your time with a focus on God's provision.

8. Conclusion/Resolution: **5 minutes**

   If there is time, have someone in the group read the Conclusion.

   Point out the importance of making a concrete resolution if we truly want to be transformed. Suggest turning the resolution into the prayer request for prayer intention time.

9. Prayer Intention Time: **15 minutes**

PASSIONATE TALK

Lesson 9

1. Social time: **10 minutes**

2. Welcome the women in your small group: **5 minutes**

3. Watch the video (stream it or use a DVD): **30 minutes**

   Point out the outline available in the book and encourage note taking during the video.

4. Small Group Discussion: **30 minutes**

   Discussion questions for the talk are found at the end of the outline in Lesson 9.

5. Prayer Intention Time: **15 minutes**

BRAVE BIBLE STUDY

Lesson 10

1. Social time: **10 minutes**

2. Opening Prayer: The Armor of God/Introduction: **10 minutes**

   After praying together, say, "Lesson 10 brings us to the final stage of our journey, the Warrior. In the words of Saint Francis of Assisi, 'We have all been called to heal wounds, to unite what has fallen apart, and to bring home those who have lost their way.' This is our mission. We don't just want to experience healing for our own sake. We want to become stronger, healthier, more passionate and mature women so that we can bring healing to others. Before we move into the lesson, did anything jump out at you from the introduction?"

3. Day One (Stand Firm): **10 minutes**

   Ask question **2A**. Read the sentence that follows, "Our job is to stand firm. God's job is to defeat the enemy."

   Summarize the following commentary by saying, "According to Saint Ignatius' discernment of spirits, the process of figuring out what the enemy is up to– what his tactics are– begins with noting what is the general direction of a person's life. Is she moving toward God or away from God? The enemy has different tactics depending on how you answer that question.

   With someone moving away from God, the enemy will do all he can to keep her comfortable and focused on pleasure. But when someone's direction is toward God, the enemy will 'bite, sadden, place obstacles and disquiet with false reasons.'"

   As you look at this lesson, can you think of any times when you have experienced this in your own life?" (The women should draw their answers from question **2**.)

   Move on to question **3** and say, "We can stand firm because the enemy is not the only one with tactics. When God is at work, what does He do? Can you see examples of Him doing this in your life?" (The women should draw their answers from question **3**.)

4. Day Two (Hold Your Ground): **10 minutes**

   Ask question **1**.

   Ask, "What are some of the other weapons we see from this lesson? We see the first in question **2**." Answer- worship

   Ask, "What is the weapon we see explored in question **3**? What resulted from Daniel's fasting and repentance?"

   Have everyone look at the *Quiet Your Heart*. Ask, "Which weapon did Saint John Bosco talk about in this section?"

5. Day Three (Armor Up): **10 minutes**

   This particular section of the study is very important to lean into. It will provide a review of much of what we've learned and will remind the women of which sections they should return to when they review these truths in the future. Now would be a good time to tell the women in your group that going through this study doesn't mean that we will never struggle to walk in freedom. We'll need to review these truths and revisit them. Their copy of *Fearless and Free* should be kept handy, and they should bookmark the parts that are especially helpful.

   Then say, "Now we'll be moving into discussing our armor. Let's look at question **1**. What should be fastened around our waist?" Allow someone to answer.

   Summarize the commentary that follows by saying, "Fastening the belt of truth means that we agree with God about what He says is true, which was a big focus in the Wakening. According to the commentary here, what did we learn from Lesson 2: Chosen?" (Answer: we learned the truth about our identity and destiny)

   "When should you revisit that lesson?" (Answer: when I start to question my worth).

   Continue by saying, "We've learned that in the battle, the enemy will attack us by distorting truth. We need to counter that with a declaration of truth. What should we turn to in our *Fearless and Free* book to help us do this?" (Answer: The "I Declares" in Appendix 5).

   "Where should we turn when we need to be reminded of our true identity as beloved daughters of God?" (Answer: "Who I Am In Christ" in Appendix 6)

Discuss **1B** with the group. After they answer, ask, "Where should we turn for additional help in gaining victory in these areas of struggle?" (Answer: Appendix 7: "Scripture Memory")

Ask question **2**. The answer is very quick ("the breastplate of righteousness"). Then ask, "In which lesson did we focus on the importance of not just knowing what is right and true, but also doing it?" (Answer: The Wrestling)

Have the women review the commentary to summarize the lessons learned in Lesson 6: Mature and Lesson 8: Passionate.

If time has run out, skip question **3** and move on to Day 4.

6. Day Four (Raise Your Sword): **10 minutes**

Ask question **1 A** and **B** and allow for quick answers. Have one of the group members read the commentary that follows.

Ask question **1 C.**

Ask question **2A, B,** and **C.** Conclude this section by reading or paraphrase the following section from the commentary, "A woman who thinks she has to be perfect to earn God's love has left her helmet of salvation on the table...confess wherever we wander."

7. Day Five (Overcome and Conquer): **10 minutes**

This day explores the power of prayer in the battle.

Ask question **1**, then skip to question **2**. Ask this question and allow discussion. Have someone in the group read the commentary that follows.

Ask question **3A** and **B**. Have someone read the quote from Peter Kreeft to share his perspective on the power of prayer.
Ask question **C** and then read the commentary that follows, stopping after reading Hebrews 12:1.

8. Conclusion/Resolution: **5 minutes**

Read the first half of the conclusion, beginning with "I wish I could promise..." and concluding with "Our King of kings and Lord of lords fights for us and never leaves our side." Point out the importance of making a concrete resolution if we truly want to be transformed. Suggest turning the resolution into the prayer request for prayer intention time.

9. Prayer Intention Time: **15 minutes**

BRAVE TALK

Lesson 11

1. Social time: **10 minutes**

2. Welcome the women in your small group: **5 minutes**

3. Watch the video (stream it or use a DVD): **30 minutes**

   Point out the outline available in the book and encourage note taking during the video.

4. Small Group Discussion: **30 minutes**

   Discussion questions for the talk are found at the end of the outline in Lesson 11.

5. Prayer Intention Time: **15 minutes**

Small Group Honor Code

At WWP, we are all about small group communities characterized by mutual encouragement and support instead of competition and comparison. We commit to living out the following values:

Confidentiality
We agree that whatever is shared here stays here. This includes what is shared through phone calls, e-mails, etc. We want this group to be a safe place to grow.

Authenticity
We will seek to be open and honest with each other. Our small group is a place to take off our masks, be ourselves, and be accepted for who we are.

Respect
We agree to communicate in ways that are respectful, and to give advice only when it is requested. We are all at various points on our spiritual journeys. We commit to giving each other grace and not throwing stones of judgment at one another.

Positivity
Negativity weighs down the heart, so we strive to communicate in a way that is filled with hope and encouragement.

A Spirit of Welcome
We agree to keep an empty chair for others and seek to reach out to other women who need this place of caring and growth.

walking with purpose

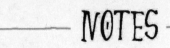

NOTES

Answer Key

NOTES

Lesson 2, Day One

1. **A.** He wrote that we are not our own; we have been purchased at a price.
   B. Answers will vary.
2. **A.** Grace and peace.
   B. Answers will vary.
3. We were chosen, in Christ, to be holy and blameless.

Lesson 2, Day Two

1. He destined us for adoption. His motive was love.
2. We can be led by the Spirit of God. This is not a spirit that causes us to fall back into fear, but one of adoption, which allows us to cry, "Abba, Father!" The Holy Spirit testifies with our spirit that we are children of God. We are also heirs of God and joint heirs with Christ, if we suffer with Him.
3. **Matthew 6:31–34** We don't need to worry about what we are going to eat, drink, or wear, because our heavenly Father knows everything we need and promises to provide it.
   Matthew 10:29–31 God cares about every detail of His daughters' lives. He has even counted every hair on our heads. Nothing touches us that escapes His notice. We are worth everything to Him.
   Romans 8:38–39 Nothing can separate us from the love of God in Christ Jesus. Nothing.
4. For the praise of the glory of His grace.

Lesson 2, Day Three

1. We have redemption by His blood, the forgiveness of transgressions, and the privilege of knowing the mystery of God's will.
2. I was ransomed with the blood of Jesus.
3. Answers will vary.
4. We are forgiven on the basis of, or according to, the riches of God's grace.
5. He's made known to us the mystery of His will—His plan for the fullness of time.

Lesson 2, Day Four

1. **A.** We are chosen and destined.
   B. He is accomplishing all things according to the intention of His will.
   C. Answers will vary.
2. He is accomplishing all things according to His will so we can exist for the praise of His glory.
3. We are sealed with the Holy Spirit.
4. **A.** He is the first installment of our inheritance.
   B. Our inheritance is described as imperishable, undefiled, and unfading, kept for us in heaven.

Lesson 2, Day Five

1. So that we would have knowledge of Jesus.
2. **A.** Hope
   B. Answers will vary.

3. **A.** Riches; glory.

B. I am blessed. I am chosen. I am adopted. I am God's beloved daughter. I am redeemed. I am forgiven. I am lavished with grace. I can know the mystery of God's will. I am a part of His great plan. I have an inheritance in heaven. I am sealed with the Holy Spirit. I am filled with the Holy Spirit. I exist for the praise of God's glory. I can come to know God personally. I have a spirit of wisdom and revelation within me—the Holy Spirit. The eyes of my heart can be enlightened. I have hope. I am God's special possession. God looks at me and feels wealthy because I belong to Him. I have access to divine power within.

4. **A.** Power

B. This same power raised Jesus from the dead.

C. Answers will vary.

1 John 4:4 "He who is in you is greater than He that is in the world."

Lesson 4, Day One

1. Ephesians 2:1 says that before we encounter Jesus, we are dead in our sins and transgressions.

2. **A.** The three forces are: the age of this world, the ruler of the power of the air, and the desires of our flesh.

B. The devil is referred to as "Satan, the Evil One, the angel who opposes God. The devil is the one who 'throws himself across' God's plan and his work of salvation accomplished in Christ."

C. The desires of the flesh are immorality, impurity, licentiousness, idolatry, sorcery, hatred, rivalry, jealousy, outbursts of fury, acts of selfishness, dissension, factions, occasions of envy, drinking bouts, and orgies.

3. **A.** Answers will vary.

B. Answers will vary.

4. **A.** **Concupiscence:** Human appetites or desires that remain disordered due to the temporal consequences of original sin, which remain even after baptism, and which produce an inclination to sin.

B. **i.** Conversion to Christ, baptism, the Holy Spirit, and the Eucharist.

ii. It didn't get rid of the frailty and weakness of our human nature, nor the inclination or bent toward sin, called "concupiscence."

iii. The struggle of conversion is directed toward holiness and eternal life.

Lesson 4, Day Two

1. **A.** We were dead through our trespasses.

B. God made us alive together with Christ and saved us by grace. He raised us up with Him, and made us sit with Him in the heavenly places in Christ Jesus.

C. We hear Jesus' word and believe in the One who sent Jesus: God. We are baptized—buried with Jesus and then raised in newness of life. "Through Baptism we are freed from sin and reborn as sons of God" (CCC 1213).

2. **A.** We are saved by grace through faith. It's a gift of God, not the result of our works.

B. Grace is favor, the free and undeserved help that God gives us to respond to His call to become His children and participate in His own divine life. Grace is the gift God makes to us of His own life, which is infused into our soul by the Holy Spirit to heal us of sin and make us more like Jesus.

3. Answers will vary.

4. We are God's handiwork, created for the good works that God has prepared in advance for us to do.

Lesson 4, Day Three

1. **A.** The Gentiles were without Christ, alienated from the community of Israel and strangers to the covenants of promise, without hope and without God in the world.
   B. The Gentiles were brought near to God by the blood of Christ.

2. Answers will vary.

3. **A.** Jesus is our peace. He made the two separate groups one, and broke down the wall that divided them. He created one new person in place of the two. He reconciled both with God through the cross. He came and preached peace to those who were far off (the Gentiles) and those who were near (the Jews), and gave *all* access to the Holy Spirit.
   B. Answers will vary.

4. So then, *I* am no longer a stranger or a sojourner. *I* am a fellow citizen with the holy ones and a member of the household of God, built upon the foundation of the apostles and prophets, with Christ Jesus Himself as the capstone. Through Him the whole structure is held together and grows into a temple sacred in the Lord; in Him *I* am being built together into a dwelling place of God in the Spirit.

Lesson 4, Day Four

1. **A.** The mystery of Christ was made known to Paul.
   B. He has made the mystery known to us. He is bringing to light the mystery hidden from ages past.
   C. The Gentiles are coheirs, members of the same body, and co-partners in the promise in Christ Jesus through the gospel.

2. He was to preach the inscrutable riches of Christ to the Gentiles and help shed light on what God's plan has been from the very beginning.

3. **A.** The manifold wisdom of God—His perfect plan—is made known through the Church to the principalities and authorities in heaven.
   B. God's plan has been to sum up all things in Christ.

4. He asked them not to lose heart over his afflictions for them—that his suffering was their glory.

Lesson 4, Day Five

1. **A.** Inner self
   B. Hearts
   C. The heart is the dwelling place where I am, where I live, where I withdraw. It's our hidden center, beyond the grasp of our reason and of others. Only the Spirit of God can fathom it and know it fully. It's the place of decision and the place of truth, where we choose life or death. It's the place of encounter with God.

2. The antidote is being rooted and grounded in love. It's being so certain of the breadth, length, height, and depth of God's love that we find our security in Him.

3. **2 Peter 3:9** He doesn't want anyone to perish. He wants everyone to come to repentance.
   Philippians 2:8 How far did He go for us? All the way to the cross.
   Romans 8:34 Jesus is loving us in heaven, where He is interceding on our behalf.
   Ephesians 4:8–9 Jesus descended into "the lower regions of the earth" out of love for us and a desire to save us all.

4. When we are rooted and grounded in Christ's love, we are filled with all the fullness of God.

Lesson 6, Day One

1. **A.** We are to be humble, gentle, and patient, bearing with one another through love. We're to strive to preserve the unity of the spirit through the bond of peace.
   B. Answers will vary.

2. **A.** He measured out the gift of grace.
   B. He gave gifts to men.
   C. He ascended and descended so He could fill all things.

3. **Evangelists:** Without the gospel, we are lost. The gospel is our starting point. It's where we recognize our need for Christ. Without an understanding of the gospel, we will fall back on ungodly self-reliance and won't move forward in maturity or healing.
   Prophets: Prophets speak the truth of what can happen in the future. Prophecy is rooted in the promises of God, proclaiming them in such a way that we can claim them and cling to them.
   Pastors: Where would we be without pastors? We need people who care for our hearts, who tend to us not just as a mass of humanity but as a smaller group of people with specific needs. Pastors shrink the larger community into groups in which authenticity and intimacy can thrive.
   Teachers: Teachers can impart wisdom, helping us to see the way our knowledge can be applied to daily life. They can educate us so that we recognize the difference between the lies of the culture and the truth of our faith.
   Apostles: Apostles can chart vision and help us see that life doesn't have to remain as it is. Their leadership can help us picture what could be. This gives us hope to journey forward toward wholeness.

4. **A.** Attaining to the unity of faith and knowledge of the Son of God, to mature manhood, to the extent of the full stature of Christ.
   B. Answers will vary.

Lesson 6, Day Two

1. **A.** They are described as being tossed by waves and swept along by every wind of teaching arising from human trickery.
   B. Answers will vary.

2. A mark of spiritual maturity is living the truth in love.

3. **A.** It says that we should stop judging, or we'll be judged. The measure with which we judge will be measured out to us.

B. Answers will vary.

4. Answers will vary.

Lesson 6, Day Three

1. They live in the futility of their minds; their understanding is darkened; they are alienated from the life of God because of ignorance and hardness of heart; they are callous; they've handed themselves over to licentiousness.

2. We are to put away the old self of our former way of life, which was corrupted through deceitful desires, and be renewed in the spirit of our minds. We are to put on the new self, created in righteousness and holiness of truth.

3. We have to "learn Christ." We need to have heard of Him and be taught in Him, because truth is found in Jesus.

4. **A.** They are not of flesh, but are enormously powerful. They are capable of destroying fortresses.

   B. We are destroying arguments and pretensions that raise themselves up against the knowledge of God.

   C. We take it captive in obedience to Christ.

Lesson 6, Day Four

1. **A.** We're told to put away falsehood and speak the truth because we're all members of the same body. In the words of theologian N. T. Wright, "Telling lies is a form of corporate self-deceit."[63]

   B. It's described as rejoicing with the truth.

   C. Answers will vary.

2. **A.** He writes that we can be angry, but we aren't to sin. We aren't to let the sun set on our anger. If we ignore these instructions, we are leaving room for the devil to come in and mess with us. It's like we're leaving the door open a crack; the results can be very damaging.

   B. No. It's possible to be angry in a holy way. Jesus displayed righteous anger when He cleansed the temple.

   C. Answers will vary.

3. Our words should edify the person we are talking to. Our words should be imparting grace.

Lesson 6, Day Five

1. **A.** We are asked not to grieve the Holy Spirit.

   B. The Holy Spirit convicts the world in regard to sin, righteousness, and condemnation.

2. **A.** We'll get rid of bitterness, fury, anger, shouting, reviling, and every form of malice.

   B. We'll be sure to be kind, compassionate, and forgiving.

   C. Answers will vary.

3. **Genesis 4:7** Sin is crouching at our door. Its desire is for us, but we must master it.

   Romans 6:12 We are not to let sin control our bodies. We are not to obey its desires.

---

[63] Wright, *Paul for Everyone*, 55.

Romans 6:16 We are slaves to whatever we obey. We can obey sin and be led to death, or we can obey God and be led to righteousness and freedom.

4. The basis for us forgiving those who have hurt us is how much Christ has forgiven in us. The more we dwell on everything His mercy has covered in our own lives, the more our hearts are tendered toward others.

Lesson 8, Day One

1. **A.** We're called to be imitators of God and live in love.
   B. It's described as a fragrant aroma.
2. **A.** If we are going to imitate God, we will be free of immorality, impurity, greed, obscenity, and silly or suggestive talk.
   B. He said that not only should these things not be found in our lives, we shouldn't even mention them.
   C. Answers will vary.
3. **A.** Answers will vary.
   B. Answers will vary.

Lesson 8, Day Two

1. **A.** We are not to be deceived by empty arguments.
   B. Answers will vary.
   C. The One who is in me, *God Himself*, is greater than he who is in the world.
2. Once we were darkness, but now we are light in the Lord. We are to live as children of light.
3. It is the Holy Spirit who enlightens and strengthens us to live as children of light. He teaches us to pray to the Father, becomes our life, and prompts us to bear the fruit of the Spirit. He challenges us to be holy. At the same time, He heals the wounds of sin and renews us on the inside through a spiritual transformation.
4. **A.** We are to "try to learn what is pleasing to the Lord, and take no part in the fruitless works of darkness; rather expose them."
   B. Answers will vary.
   C. Answers will vary.

Lesson 8, Day Three

1. **A.** We will make the most of every opportunity; we will try to understand the Lord's will; we'll be filled with the Spirit; we'll address one another in psalms, hymns, and spiritual songs; we'll sing and play to the Lord and always give thanks for everything.
   B. We will not live as foolish persons. We won't continue in ignorance. We won't get drunk on wine.
2. **A.** Answers will vary.
   B. Answers will vary.
3. **A.** We are told to avoid getting drunk on wine. The alternative is to be filled with the Spirit.
   B. **John 14:15–18, 26** He is our counselor and our advocate. He leads us into truth and dwells within us. He teaches us everything and reminds us of everything that Jesus has taught.

Romans 8:26 He comes to the aid of our weakness. He intercedes within us in prayer.

Acts 1:8 He fills us with power.

2 Corinthians 3:17 Where the Spirit of the Lord is, there is freedom.

4. We ask God to give us the Holy Spirit. He will not say no.

Lesson 8, Day Four

1. We are all to be subordinate to one another, out of reverence for Christ.

   1 Corinthians 13:5 When we are mutually submissive to one another, we aren't seeking our own interests. This means we aren't rude, quick-tempered, or brooding over our injuries.

   Galatians 5:13 We are to serve one another in love.

   Philippians 2:3–4 We are to do nothing out of selfish ambition or vain conceit, but in humility we are to consider others more important than ourselves. Instead of looking out for our own interests, we are to look to the interests of others.

2. She is to be subordinate to him, seeing him as the head of the family, just as Christ is the head of the Church. Just as the Church submits to Christ, wives should submit to their husbands.

3. Husbands are to love their wives as Christ loved the Church. They are to be willing to sacrifice everything for their wives.

4. Answers will vary.

Lesson 8, Day Five

1. **A.** Children are to obey their parents and to honor their father and mother.

   B. We are to leave our mother and father and be joined to our spouse.

   C. Answers will vary.

   D. Answers will vary.

2. Answers will vary.

3. **Psalm 68:6 (NAB)** God is the Father of the fatherless.

   Romans 8:35–39 Nothing can separate us from the love of God.

   Philippians 4:19 God will supply all your needs according to His glorious riches in Christ Jesus.

4. Answers will vary. Whatever we do for even the "least of these," Jesus sees that we have really done it for Him.

Lesson 10, Day One

1. We are to draw our strength from the Lord and from His mighty power. Instead of doing this, we often resort to ungodly self-reliance. We press the "dig deeper" button and force ourselves to keep going. We grit our teeth and persevere. But this response is not only unsustainable, it harms us on the soul level, leading us to sin.

2. **A.** So that we may be able to stand firm against the tactics of the devil.

   B. A biting that unsettles: Answers will vary.

   Sadness: Answers will vary.

   Obstacles: Answers will vary.

   Disquiet with false reasons: Answers will vary.

3. God consoles. Answers will vary.
   God strengthens. Answers will vary.
   God inspires. Answers will vary.
   God removes obstacles. Answers will vary.
   Answers will vary.
4. Our struggle is with the principalities, the powers, the world rulers of this present darkness, and the evil spirits in the heavens.
   Answers will vary.

Lesson 10, Day Two

1. We're told to put on the armor of God. Having done everything, we're told to hold our ground.
2. He holds his head high above his enemies on every side. He offers sacrifices with shouts of joy and sings and chants praise to God.
3. **Isaiah 58:6** Authentic fasting releases those bound unjustly and unties the thongs of the yoke. It sets the oppressed free.
   Daniel 9:3, 21–23 Daniel prayed and fasted, and in response, the angel Gabriel (and later the archangel Michael, as seen in Daniel 10:12–13) came to his aid.

Lesson 10, Day Three

1. **A.** The belt of truth should be around your waist.
   B. Answers will vary.
2. **A.** We are to put on the breastplate of righteousness.
   B. Answers will vary.
3. **A.** Our feet are to be shod in readiness for the gospel of peace.
   B. Answers will vary.
   1 Peter 3:15 "Always be prepared to give an answer to everyone who asks you to give the reason for the hope that you have. But do this with gentleness and respect."
   Before Jesus . . . Answers will vary.
   I encountered Christ personally in this way . . . Answers will vary.
   This is the difference He has made . . . Answers will vary.

Lesson 10, Day Four

1. **A.** We are to hold faith as a shield to quench the flaming arrows of the evil one.
   B. Hebrews 11:1 tells us that faith is confidence in what we hope for and assurance about what we do not see. Hebrews 11:6 teaches that without faith it is impossible to please God, because anyone who comes to Him must believe that He exists and that He rewards those who earnestly seek Him.
   C. Answers will vary.
2. **A.** Our heads should be covered by the helmet of salvation.
   B. **Mark 16:16** The one who believes and is baptized will be saved.
   Acts 2:21 If we call on the name of the Lord, we will be saved.
   CCC 977 Our Lord tied the forgiveness of sins (essential for salvation) to faith and baptism.

C. We are forgiven and reconciled with God and the Church through the sacrament of penance.

3. A. Our offensive weapon is the sword of the Spirit—the Word of God.

B. A sharp, two-edged sword was coming out of His mouth.

C. The Word of God is living and active, sharper than any two-edged sword, piercing until it divides soul from spirit, joints from marrow; it is able to judge the thoughts and intentions of the heart.

Lesson 10, Day Five

1. 2 Chronicles 7:14 When we pray, we need to start by humbling ourselves. Then we need to seek God's face, focusing on Him, not our difficulties. Lastly, this verse tells us that we have to turn from our wicked ways. This means we walk away from sinful behavior instead of justifying it.

Psalm 66:18 Unconfessed sin blocks our prayers.

1 John 5:14 Our prayers should be run by the litmus test of whether they are in sync with God's will. If we don't know—which is often the case—we can end our prayer by asking that ultimately God's will would be done.

2. Answers will vary.

3. A. The angel Gabriel set out from the first day that Daniel made up his mind to gain understanding and to humble himself. He came in response to Daniel's prayer.

B. The prince of the kingdom of Persia opposed the angel Gabriel for twenty-one days. Michael the archangel came to help Gabriel, and was left there battling with the prince of the kingdom of Persia.

C. made up your mind/understanding/humble yourself

NOTES

Prayer Pages

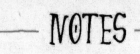

NOTES

The Armor of God

May we be strong in the Lord and in the strength of your power.

May we put on the full armor of God,
so we may be able to stand against the wiles of the devil.

For our struggle is not against enemies of blood and flesh, but against the
rulers, against the authorities, against the cosmic powers of this present
darkness, against the spiritual forces of evil in the heavenly places.

So may we take up the whole armor of God, so we may be able to
withstand everything, and having done everything, to stand firm.
May we stand and fasten the belt of truth around our waists.

May we put on the breastplate of righteousness.

May our shoes make us ready to proclaim the gospel of peace.

May we take up the shield of faith,
and use it to quench all the flaming arrows of the evil one.

May we take the helmet of salvation and the sword of the Spirit,
which is the Word of God.

May we pray in the Spirit at all times.

May we keep alert and always persevere in prayer.
Amen.

Prayer Requests

Date:

Date:

Prayer Requests

Date:

Date:

Prayer Requests

Date:

Date:

Prayer Requests

Date:

Date:

Prayer Requests

Date:

Date:

Prayer Requests

Date:

Date:

NOTES

"For to the one who has, more will be given"
Matthew 13:12

CHRIST'S LOVE IS ENDLESS.

And the journey doesn't end here.

Walking With Purpose is more than a Bible study, it's a supportive community of women seeking lasting transformation of the heart. And you are invited.

Walking With Purpose believes that change happens in the hearts of women – and, by extension, in their families and beyond – through Bible study and community. We welcome all women, irrespective of faith background, age, or marital status.

Connect with us online for regular inspiration and to join the conversation. There you'll find insightful blog posts, Scriptures, and downloads.

For a daily dose of spiritual nourishment, join our community on Facebook, Twitter, Pinterest and Instagram.

And if you're so moved to start a Walking With Purpose study group at home or in your parish, take a look at our website for more information.

walkingwithpurpose.com
The Modern Woman's Guide to the Bible.

walking with purpose

 NOTES

NOTES

# NOTES

NOTES

 NOTES

NOTES

NOTES

NOTES

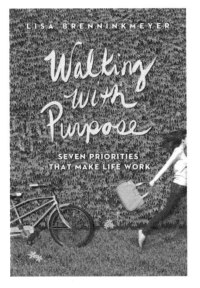

⚘ DEEPEN YOUR FAITH ⚘ OPEN YOUR ARMS ⚘ ⚘ BROADEN YOUR CIRCLE ⚘

When your heart opens, and your love for Christ deepens, you may be moved to bring Walking With Purpose to your friends or parish. It's rewarding experience for many women who, in doing so, learn to rely on God's grace while serving Him.

If leading a group seems like a leap of faith, consider that you already have all the skills you need to share the Lord's Word:

- Personal commitment to Christ
- Desire to share the love of Christ
- Belief in the power of authentic, transparent community

The Walking With Purpose community supports you with:

- Training
- Mentoring
- Bible study materials
- Promotional materials

Few things stretch and grow our faith like stepping out of our comfort zone and asking God to work through us. Say YES, soon you'll see the mysterious and unpredictable ways He works through imperfect women devoted to Him.

Remember that if you humbly offer Him what you can, He promises to do the rest.

"See to it that no one misses the grace of God" Hebrews 12:15

**Learn more about bringing Walking with Purpose to your parish.
Visit us at walkingwithpurpose.com
The Modern Woman's Guide To The Bible.**

INTRODUCING **blaze** THE MODERN GIRL'S GUIDE TO THE BIBLE.

Do you want to help girls grow in confidence, faith, and kindness?

The Lord is calling for women like you to speak truth into the hearts of young girls – girls who are understandably confused about their true worth and beauty. Blaze is a fun and engaging program developed especially for 7th and 8th grade girls to counteract the cultural forces that drive them to question their value, purpose, and faith.

Like Walking With Purpose, Blaze makes the wisdom of the Bible relevant to today's challenges. Blaze teaches girls to recognize the difference between the loving, affirming voice of their heavenly Father and the voices that tell them they aren't good enough.

Would you like to be a positive influence on the girls you know? Start a Blaze program in in your parish or community.

It's easy and convenient to share God's word with a Leader's Guide and Blaze kit that includes:

- Blaze Prayer Journals
- Truth vs. Lie Cards
- Fun gifts for the girls
- Facebook and Instagram messaging to maintain connection and amplify the message

Additional resources to nurture girls' spiritual growth:

- Discovering My Purpose – a 6-session Bible study that leads girls on an exploration of their own spiritual gifts
- Between You & Me – a 40-day conversation guide for mothers and daughters

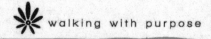 walking with purpose

For more spiritual inspiration or to learn more about Blaze and Walking With Purpose, visit us at walkingwithpurpose.com/BLAZE

You're also invited to join our community on Facebook, Twitter, Pinterest and Instagram.

"Be who God meant you to be and you will set the world on fire." - Saint Catherine of Siena

THE GUIDED TOUR OF GOD'S LOVE BEGINS HERE.

Opening Your Heart: The Starting Point begins a woman's exploration of her Catholic faith and enhances her relationship with Jesus Christ. This Bible study is designed to inspire thoughtful consideration of the fundamental questions of living a life in the Lord. More than anything, it's a weekly practice of opening your heart to the only One who can heal and transform lives.

Explore these topics and more:

- What is the role of the Holy Spirit in my life?
- What does the Eucharist have to do with my friendship with Christ?
- What are the limits of Christ's forgiveness?
- Why and how should I pray?
- What is the purpose of suffering?
- What challenges will I face in my efforts to follow Jesus more closely?
- How can fear be overcome?

A companion DVD series complements this journey with practical insights and spiritual support.

Opening Your Heart is a foundational 22-week Bible study that serves any woman who seeks to grow closer to God. It's an ideal starting point for women who are new to Walking with Purpose, and those with prior practice in Bible study, too.

To share Walking with Purpose with the women in your parish, contact us at walkingwithpurpose.com/start.

Walking With Purpose
The modern woman's guide to the Bible.
walkingwithpurpose.com

walking with purpose

These transformative full-length Bible studies are created to help women deepen their personal relationship with Christ. Each study includes many lessons that explore core themes and challenges of modern life through the ancient wisdom of the Bible and the Catholic Church.

INTRODUCTORY LEVEL

Opening Your Heart

A thoughtful consideration of the fundamental questions of faith – from why and how to pray to the role of the Holy Spirit in our lives and the purpose of suffering.

Living In the Father's Love

Gain a deeper understanding of how God's unconditional love transforms your relationship with others, with yourself, and most dearly, with Him.

INTERMEDIATE LEVEL

Keeping in Balance

Discover how the wisdom of the Old and New Testaments can help you live a blessed lifestyle of calm, health, and holiness.

Touching the Divine

These thoughtful studies draw you closer to Jesus and deepen your faith, trust, and understanding of what it means to be God's beloved daughter.

Discovering Our Dignity

Modern-day insight directly from women of the Bible presented as a tender, honest, and loving conversation–woman to woman.

Beholding His Glory

Old Testament Scripture leads us directly to our Redeemer, Jesus Christ. Page after page, God's awe-inspiring majesty is a treasure to behold.

Beholding Your King

This study of King David and several Old Testament prophets offers a fresh perspective of how all Scripture points to the glorious coming of Christ.

Grounded In Hope

Anchor yourself in the truth found in the New Testament book of Hebrews, and gain practical insight to help you run your race with perseverance.

Fearless and Free

This study is for any woman confronting the reality that life isn't easy through compassionate lessons to flourish in Christ's love.

Walking With Purpose is a supportive community of women seeking lasting transformation of the heart through Bible study. We welcome all women, irrespective of faith, background, age, or marital status. For a daily dose of spiritual nourishment, join our community on Facebook, Twitter, Pinterest and Instagram.

walkingwithpurpose.com

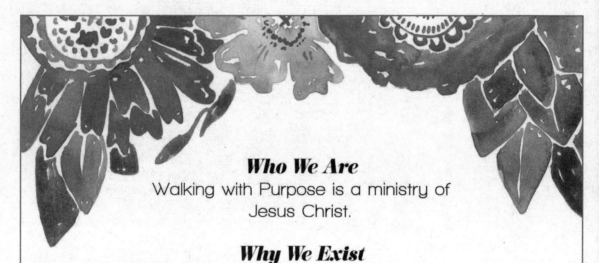

Who We Are
Walking with Purpose is a ministry of
Jesus Christ.

Why We Exist
We exist to enable women to know Jesus Christ
personally through Scripture and the teachings of the
Roman Catholic Church.

Our Mission
Our mission is to help every American Catholic woman
and girl to open her heart to Jesus Christ.

Our Vision
Our vision for the future is that, as more Catholic women
deepen their relationships with Jesus Christ, eternity-
changing transformation will take place in their hearts –
and, by extension – in their families, in their communities,
and ultimately, in our nation.

walking with purpose